Trauma-Responsive Pedagogy

NOT THIS ● BUT THAT

Trauma-Responsive Pedagogy
Teaching for Healing and Transformation

ARLÈNE ELIZABETH CASIMIR
AND
COURTNEY N. BAKER

HEINEMANN
PORTSMOUTH, NH

Heinemann
145 Maplewood Avenue, Suite 300
Portsmouth, NH 03801
www.heinemann.com

The authors and publisher wish to thank those who have generously given permission to reprint borrowed material:

[Sect 1, p. 6] Excerpt from "Responsive Schools: Building a Trauma Responsive Learning Community for All Children" by Barbara Pierce, Megan Carlson, and Wanda Thruston. Published by Clinical Scholars. Reprinted by permission of the publisher.

[Sect 2, p. 24] Reprinted from *American Journal of Preventive Medicine*, Vol. 14, No. 4, Vincent Felitti, Robert F. Anda, Dale Nordenberg, David F. Williamson, Alison M. Spitz, Valerie Edwards, Mary P. Koss, James S. Marks, "Relationship of Childhood Abuse and Household Dysfunction to Many of the Leading Causes of Death in Adults: The Adverse Childhood Experiences (ACE) Study," pp. 248–258, Copyright 1998, with permission from Elsevier Science.

Credits continue on page vi

ISBN: 978-0-325-13414-7
Library of Congress Control Number: 2023903045

Acquisitions Editor: Margaret LaRaia
Series Editors: Nell K. Duke and M. Colleen Cruz
Editors: Louisa Irele and Tobey Antao
Production Editors: Kimberlee Sims and Sonja Chapman
Cover and Interior Designer: Monica Ann Cohen
Typesetter: Valerie Levy Drawing Board Studios
Manufacturing: Val Cooper, Jaime Spaulding

Printed in the United States of America on acid-free paper
2 3 4 5 6 VP 28 27 26 25 24
February, 2024, PO4500883355

CONTENTS

....

INTRODUCTION

Nell K. Duke

If you have been in education for a while, you have no doubt seen certain areas get lots of attention for a short period of time and then fade from the spotlight. For example, when I was a teacher in training, cooperative learning was all the rage. Over decades, research continues to document the benefits of cooperative learning in numerous domains and at a wide range of age/grade levels, but the technique is far less commonly discussed and is probably underutilized.

I have been worried that trauma-responsive education may experience the same fate. There was a meteoric rise in attention to this topic, begun prior to the pandemic and then magnified during the pandemic. Yet already it seems as though this topic is fading from view in favor of others, such as "accelerated learning." I am hoping that educators passionate about the important role that mental health plays in learning, and compassionate for children and youth who have experienced trauma, will help keep this topic front and center. And I hope that this brilliant book will play a role.

Another worry I have related to trauma-responsive education is that our field will attempt to enact it without sufficiently aligning to research. The rapidity with which trauma-responsive education has become known, and the many other demands that have co-occurred with that rise (e.g., figuring out how to teach remotely), make trauma-responsive education vulnerable to implementation that is underinformed by research. This is one reason why this book is so needed. It is short and accessible, which is key given so many demands on our time and thinking. Yet it also covers many important findings from research and expert practice.

This book addresses another worry I have had about trauma-responsive education: lack of an equity lens. The field needs to recognize the roles that systemic racism and classism in the United States play both in causing trauma and in affecting the degree to which schooling is responsive to trauma. At the same time, we must be vigilant that awareness of trauma does not lead to lower expectations for children who have experienced trauma or to excuse ourselves from providing all children a culturally and intellectually rigorous and engaging curriculum. I am grateful that in this book, discussion of trauma always includes attention to issues of equity.

To write this book, we needed authors who know research and practice in this area well. Arlène Elizabet Casimir was a clear choice. She used trauma-responsive practices as a classroom teacher, then in curriculum development work, and now as a professional developer and coach. Throughout her work, she thoroughly resists the deficit orientation that is so common in conversations about trauma and trauma-responsive instruction. Arlène is in enormous demand, and I could not be more thankful that she has decided to share her expertise and commitments in this book.

Courtney N. Baker, too, has a long history of work on trauma-responsive practice. Her research investigates approaches to providing trauma-responsive educational experiences for children, youth, and families. She has led numerous projects in this area, working in partnership with community and education organizations. Like Arlène, she brings an asset orientation to the work that is so important to progress in this area. Please join us in making that progress, appreciate what Arlène and Courtney have written, and thank yourselves for all you are doing to support children and youth who have experienced trauma.

LETTER TO READERS

Dear Reader,

We are so grateful that you are here with us to learn more about trauma-responsive pedagogy. Welcome!

Growing poverty and income inequality, social injustice, and system inequality, coupled with the global COVID-19 pandemic, mean that more children are attending school every year who have experienced significant chronic and acute stressors. Educators like you are deeply interested in supporting students, helping them learn, and ensuring that they reach their full potential. Trauma-informed schools are lauded as one way to address this challenge, but the concept can be challenging to define and difficult for teachers to implement, especially on their own. Together, we invite you, our reader, to explore the research and practice of trauma-responsive pedagogy in an easy-to-digest, actionable text that elevates the healing and wellness of both the children and the adults in your classroom.

We met in New Orleans, Louisiana. Arlène was teaching the first children to come to school post–Hurricane Katrina, and Courtney was a founding member of the New Orleans Trauma-Informed Schools Learning Collaborative, which developed and now implements trauma-informed approaches both in New Orleans and nationally. When Arlène's school participated in the pilot of this initiative, her classroom served as a lab site and model for transformative trauma-informed teaching. She received tools from the Learning Collaborative that supported her in shaping her approach to trauma-responsive pedagogy. Since then, Courtney's journey has been to gather and share the evidence behind trauma-informed approaches, with a focus on measurement, implementation processes, and outcomes. Arlène's path has focused on educator training with an emphasis on trauma-responsive pedagogy. We came back together to write this book to share our collective knowledge and wisdom with educators.

This innovative book first describes the challenges of a classroom that does not attend to adversity and trauma, then presents the research on trauma-responsive classrooms, and finally provides a framework to support educators in centering the whole child in their classrooms. We use approachable language, provide examples and anecdotes, and share strategies and lessons. Our goal is for you to pick up, digest, and apply this text with ease.

In this book, we empower you to support children who have experienced adversity and trauma so that they can be successful, both in your classroom and out of it. Just as we hope this book will give you valuable tools to help your students, we also aspire to offer you space and an urgent rationale to care for and love yourself in this work—your empathy, kindness, generosity of spirit, and engagement are exactly what your students, school, and community need to thrive. So, please take a deep and cleansing breath, and feel deeply welcomed to join us for a process of reflection, learning, and growth. We are absolutely certain that your effort will pay transformative and worthwhile dividends.

With love and care as you embark on this most important of journeys,
—*Arlène and Courtney*

SECTION **1**

NOT ● THIS

Schools as Places That Cause Trauma

ARLÈNE ELIZABETH CASIMIR

An Invitation for Educators

Imagine going to school one morning, in person or remotely. Maybe you had an awful night, a rough week, a couple of trying weeks, or you continue to carry the weight of the global pandemic as the effects rage onward. You may be caring for an ill family member, grieving a recent loss, experiencing financial difficulty, coping with a personal health crisis, or running on limited sleep. Whatever "it" is, you are managing multiple priorities and feeling overwhelmed and stressed out as the school day begins. Picture yourself carrying this load, on your face, in your rounded shoulders, or within your spirit when you enter your school community. Now, imagine your administrator or colleagues greeting you with:

> "Good vibes only here!"
>   or
> "Fix your face and leave it at the door!"
>   or
> "You need to be positive!"
>   or
> "Show some grit!"

Or maybe no one greets you at all but, you see your name removed from the "good" green zone to the "cautionary" yellow zone on the behavior chart *for everyone to see*!

Imagine being told to control your emotions by holding a bubble in your mouth, walking like a "delighted duck," or worse, smiling and feeling "ecstatic" because *that* is the feeling the class will "study" today.

3

As you imagine this scenario, do you find yourself wondering: Where is the space for my humanity? This is a question that many students and teachers alike ask themselves every day (Shalaby 2017). It is no secret that we live in a world where people experience trauma—individually and collectively. We can consider trauma a universal human experience, given how many of us experience some, or multiple, forms of it in our lifetime. From grief and loss of those closest to us to disaster and war on a global scale, trauma impacts our lives and the lives of our students. We must also acknowledge that there are many instances where systemic injustices perpetuate trauma by way of oppression. Classism, racism, sexism, xenophobia, homophobia, and transphobia, to name a few, are connected to psychological trauma that individuals and communities experience (Holmes et al. 2016). It is important to recognize that trauma is not simply a negative experience students and teachers bring to school. There are many instances where, like many other institutions, schools can perpetuate trauma and often *are* sites of trauma themselves (Venet 2021; Duane 2022). Given these realities, I expand on what Richards (2020) wonders: Is it possible for educators and students to bring all of who they are into the classroom and still feel invited to be seen, heard, and supported through all the critical challenges that they have to navigate in life and in school?

> *Do you find yourself wondering: Where is the space for my humanity? This is a question that many students and teachers alike ask themselves every day.*

Like in the imagination exercise at the beginning of this chapter, too often educators tell our students to leave their problems at the door, be positive, and bring good vibes only. Should a student choose not to, they endure consequences for their "non-compliant behavior" such as time out of the classroom, suspensions, and expulsions. Instead of being encouraged and supported to authentically feel the vastness of their emotions and to move through them with compassion, children, particularly children of color, are often hyper surveilled, criminalized, and dehumanized (Basile et al. 2019; Morris 2016). Trauma-informed educational practice is a decentralized movement (Duane and Venet 2022) to help us consider how trauma impacts our students.

There have been many versions and iterations of this approach both within education and in other fields such as psychology, social work, and medicine (Thomas et al. 2019). However, although most versions of trauma-informed practice focus on understanding and being informed by behavioral manifestations of trauma in school settings, I argue that trauma-responsive pedagogy invites educators to go a step further and to heal alongside our students, both onstage (while explicitly integrating teaching methods and practice) and offstage (by doing the necessary inner work to bring our whole being to the profession in healthy ways). As we explore the core tenets of trauma-responsive pedagogy in Section 3, we can also recognize that this responsiveness requires individuals to take up healing-centered (Ginwright 2018) and humanizing (Freire 1964) approaches to teaching and learning. Trauma-responsive pedagogy is a *pedagogy* grounded in teachers displaying humanization. It is a *pedagogy* that can equip educators with the mindset to transform learning experiences. It is a *pedagogy* that can encourage students to turn their wounds into wisdom (Dutro 2011) and recognize that our students' challenges are not a deterrent to their learning. As you will further see in Section 3 through lesson plans and classroom examples, this pedagogical stance provides the needed insight to understand adult and child trauma and encourages healing alongside our students.

Trauma-responsive pedagogy invites educators to go a step further and to heal alongside our students.

As we support students with developing the awareness, capacities, knowledge, and skills to identify, witness, transmute, and transcend their pain, we honor their dignity and their humanity, and we even have a powerfully vulnerable opportunity to heal with them. History has shown us that we are capable of accomplishing greatness even in the midst of immense sorrow and trials (Pat-Horenczyk and Brom 2007). Trauma, and the growth that can come in its wake, is what makes us human. But our ability to embody our full humanity and to integrate our growth to propel our lives forward depends on how our community engages with the complexity and fullness of our presence.

We are capable of accomplishing greatness even in the midst of immense sorrow.

As educators, we want what's best for our students. And we have a vision for what that looks like. To support our students in more closely connecting with the vision that we cocreate for their learning experience, we make statements and decisions that we believe will help our students. However, our well-intentioned efforts can—and often do—cause harm. While administrators and teachers, for example, ask students to comply with the upbeat ideal to "show some grit" or "be positive!", we simultaneously punish children for failure to adhere (Love 2019). In doing so, we may unconsciously, or consciously, shame students for their trauma responses and perhaps cause retraumatization.

Setting the Stage: Arlène's Journey to Trauma-Responsive Pedagogy

The most efficient avenue to address childhood trauma and provide opportunities for healthy development for all children is through the public school system. This is because the vast majority of US children . . . attend public schools. Currently no other US institution has an existing and accessible structure to have such direct, long-term access to children during the thirteen crucial developmental years.
(Carlson, Pierce, and Thurston 2020, 2)

I began my teaching career in 2009 as a middle school English language arts and social justice teacher in New York City. In 2011, I moved to New Orleans, Louisiana. During the years I spent among students whose experience was shaped by trauma that existed pre– and post–Hurricane Katrina, I "grew up" as an educator and began forming my identity as a teacher. As a result of my time there, my approach to supporting schools and teachers became further grounded in equity and social justice. I left New Orleans in 2016 to work throughout the nation and world as an educational consultant in content area literacy, culturally relevant pedagogy (Ladson-Billings 1995), social-emotional learning, and trauma-informed practice.

When I branched out as a teacher-educator, I noticed that children who experienced trauma were often treated like they had a scarlet letter *T* embroidered on the chest of their clothing or like they were carrying a bindle of trauma that embarrassed and inconvenienced their classroom communities. I would hear things like "These are our struggling babies," or "These are our traumatized kids," or even worse, "These are the basket cases." These assumptions were gut wrenching to say the least. They were also shocking to me because I spent years learning how to become trauma informed at New Orleans Trauma Informed Learning Collaborative/Tulane. It was important for me to remember how I grew to understand the problematic nature of these kinds of mindsets to help teachers and administrators disrupt them. Initially, I wondered: Where is the trauma-informed professional development? Why are children's personal circumstances being used against them, and why are we acting like schools are not a place that can cause trauma? Despite my wonderings, this work always seemed pushed to the back burner—there were more pressing priorities. Yet no matter how antibiased, culturally relevant, or progressive we tried to be, the school's, students', and teachers' trauma was always the elephant or menacing shadow in the room. It proved ineffective to help one receptive teacher become trauma informed because that classroom would simply turn into an island in a sea of trauma. It was often only a matter of time before that teacher sunk into the depths of the crises in the school, grew stagnant, or left the place all together. It became clear that trying to implement trauma-informed classroom practices, "without first implementing school-wide trauma-informed organizational culture change, [was] like throwing seeds on dry land" (Bloom as quoted in Menschner and Maul [2016]). It could help a teacher—and doing so certainly helped to make that classroom an oasis in the storm of life and in the chaos of oppressive school culture—but it was not sustainable for one teacher to do this alone without the support of the entire community.

Then, our world shifted in 2020. All of a sudden, educators everywhere started to realize that everyone's collective and personal trauma was emerging. It was time for a reckoning. In the silence and

Our world shifted in 2020. All of a sudden, educators everywhere started to realize that everyone's collective and personal trauma emerged.

isolation of the global pandemic, we were forced to look within and grapple with what was not working in our lives, educational system, and society at large. I had been there before, in New Orleans, a place that faced a slew of problems that felt more fitting for a developing nation than for a part of the United States. When racial, social, and economic issues bubbled up at the height of the pandemic, I started to receive many invitations to share my experiences, research, and wisdom. Schools began to realize that to move forward, they had to heal.

The demand for trauma-responsive work has grown significantly. For myself, and other professionals who are engaged in supporting educators and schools in being trauma responsive, there has never been a more important time. It is also true that the demand for your knowledge and expertise has never been greater. Courtney and I wrote this book with the strong desire to support you as you develop even greater knowledge and expertise about trauma-responsive pedagogy.

How We Can Miss the Trauma

Like many teachers, I wanted to have strong classroom management so that I could teach academic content that could help my students decide what kind of people they wanted to be in the world. This meant I wanted students to control themselves. There I was, in a classroom in New Orleans, sitting on a carpet with twenty-eight fourth graders, all of whom were grappling with personal, racial, societal, and/or communal trauma. Oftentimes, their trauma exposure responses interrupted our lessons and took us off course. It's easy to get very discouraged and frustrated by our students' pain. But as teachers, we need to recognize that once you can help a child to name the emotions and the trauma response, you can support them to move through it with acceptance, compassion, and grace. With research, practice, and time, I developed an understanding of what I was seeing and began thinking about how to teach into the phenomenon of children expressing their trauma responses in the classroom. I began to notice a gamut of trauma responses and how they manifested for students behaviorally, cognitively, physically, interpersonally, and emotionally (Center for Substance Abuse Treatment 2014).

In past scientific research, scholars believed that there were only two universal responses to stress and trauma: fight or flight (McEwen 2007). Clinicians and practitioners have since discovered additional manifestations of trauma, such as "friend" and "freeze" (Seng et al. 2019). Figure 1–1 is a framework I've developed through years of my lived experience and learning alongside children and adults to comprise an application and extension of those ideas and how they might show up in educational settings, as well as how we might misread them.

For more research about trauma responses, see Section 3.

Figure 1–1 The "9 Fs" of Student Trauma Manifestations

POSSIBLE RESPONSE	MANIFESTATIONS	SCHOOL-SPECIFIC SCENARIOS	HOW THEY MIGHT BE MISREAD
Fight	▶ Anger ▶ Aggression ▶ Argumentative ▶ Confrontational ▶ Explosive	▶ Hitting ▶ Overreacting ▶ Throwing things ▶ Yelling ▶ A confrontational nature	We may misread this behavior as the child being "aggressive," "bad," emotionally disturbed, or having oppositional defiant disorder.
Flight	▶ Anxiety ▶ Panic attacks ▶ Paranoia ▶ Feeling trapped ▶ Escaping without a word ▶ A runner	▶ Fidgeting ▶ Constantly asking to go to the bathroom or looking for excuses to leave the room ▶ Leaving the room without a warning or a word	We may misread this behavior as a child being distracting to other students, off task, unfocused, and presenting a dangerous potential to run away.

(continues)

(continued)

POSSIBLE RESPONSE	MANIFESTATIONS	SCHOOL-SPECIFIC SCENARIOS	HOW THEY MIGHT BE MISREAD
Freeze	▶ Confusion ▶ Dissociation ▶ Hiding ▶ Numbing ▶ Spacing out ▶ Procrastination	▶ Appearing shut down or withdrawn ▶ Physically slow moving ▶ Nonresponsive	We may misread this behavior as a child being spaced out, emotionally distanced, cold, and depressed.
Faint	▶ Shutting down emotionally, mentally, spiritually, and physically	▶ Passing out ▶ Napping ▶ Placing head down on table ▶ Confusion	We may misread this student as disengaged, ill, tired, and seeking unnecessary attention.
Fawn	▶ People-pleasing or being overly accommodating ▶ Fears disappointing others by saying no ▶ Neglecting personal needs to be accepted by others ▶ Perspective taking to a fault ▶ Superpolite ▶ Betrays needs and self	▶ May not go to the bathroom even if they need to go ▶ Always offering to help ▶ May have a very strong social awareness and be hyperaware of others' emotions and needs before their own ▶ May be behind on their own work and still willing to help others to be accepted	We may misread them as either annoying, a tattletale, or on the other hand as helpful, supersweet, a teacher's pet.
Forget	▶ Loses materials ▶ Misremembers next steps for improvement plans ▶ Avoids situations that could lead to conflict ▶ Lets others make decisions	▶ Never brings their materials ▶ Does not remember the intervention that you've given ▶ May seem disorganized	We may read them as having ADD, ADHD, not wanting to learn, not caring about school, and even as disrespectful for dismissing interventions that we have put into place to help them succeed.

POSSIBLE RESPONSE	MANIFESTATIONS	SCHOOL-SPECIFIC SCENARIOS	HOW THEY MIGHT BE MISREAD
Front	▸ Posturing, or putting on a persona of toughness	▸ May come off as stoic and have a poker face ▸ Does not see others, especially adults, as trustworthy ▸ Does not show an emotional response to emotional stimuli	We may misread them as strong and not in need of compassion, empathy, and tenderness.
Fool (note: this is a verb, not a noun)	▸ Laughs at inappropriate times and in inappropriate places ▸ Has nervous laughter ▸ Laughs to keep from crying	▸ May come off as the class joker ▸ Insensitive and even cruel	We may misread them as immature, insensitive, and out of touch.
Friend	▸ Trauma bonding, or forming relationships based on similar harmful experiences ▸ Engaging with people who repeatedly cause harm ▸ Maintaining relationships based on "what's wrong" ▸ Stockholm syndrome	▸ May seem stuck in friendships that are "bad" for them but see no way of getting out ▸ Friendships based on constantly discussing and reliving traumatic events ▸ Lack of healthy boundaries in social relationships	We may think these friends are "supporting" one another. However, they may be circling in a toxic cycle of trauma, forcing students to constantly repeat it.

I want to emphasize that Figure 1–1 is *not* a checklist or a tool to label children. These responses are verbs, not nouns. My hope is that this figure serves as a resource for educators to identify and learn the manifestations of students' trauma responses. If, as teachers, we are not able to correctly identify a trauma response, we may react as if the student is behaving that way on purpose. We may turn to restricting privileges, detention or time-outs, and other punishments that don't address the root cause of the student's action or support them through their challenges.

> *Children are unable to absorb and process what we are trying to teach if their brain is busy worrying about their safety.*

We may even label the student as a "bad kid" and subconsciously treat them as such. Students are very perceptive and aware of how we feel about their trauma. They know when our classrooms and lesson plans do not have space for them to explore their responses, to integrate them, and to heal. The problem? Although social-emotional learning may seem disconnected from academic content, the two are deeply interconnected. When a student is exhibiting a trauma response, it overwhelms "the ordinary systems of care that give people a sense of control, connection, and meaning" (Herman 1992, 33). In a word, children are unable to absorb and process what we are trying to teach if their brain is busy worrying about their safety.

Now that we understand how trauma can appear in ourselves, our colleagues, families, and our students, we can identify the ways we may intentionally or unintentionally punish children for their trauma responses. Figure 1–2 offers examples of how students can be punished for potential trauma responses. These kinds of statements send messages about who we want students to be instead of accepting who they are and the reality they bring to the classroom. As a result, they can end up retraumatizing the students instead of supporting them through challenges.

A lot of these responses come from a place of feeling overwhelmed with mandates and the shifting nature of educating our students. And these statements don't only happen when our students stand in front of us. Many of us said things such as, "Turn

FIGURE 1-2 Ways We May Consciously and Unconsciously Punish Students for Their Trauma Responses While Simultaneously Retraumatizing Them

OUR STATEMENTS EXPLAINED	OUR IMPACT
"You're not able to focus; you can't sit still; why can't you write? Everyone else is writing."	▶ Calls attention to students in a potentially humiliating way ▶ Dismisses the possibility of neurodiversity ▶ Holds students accountable to speak to issues they may not be able to understand themselves ▶ Uses students' weaknesses against them ▶ Puts some students in competition with their classmates for what may be out of their control
"I am not a psychologist. I am not a social worker. My job is to teach you, not be your therapist. It's not my problem that you didn't eat! It's not my problem that you're living in an unstable home! It's not my problem that you've been absent for all these days! It's not my problem that your assignment is late!"	▶ Deflects the teacher's responsibility to cultivate caring relationships with students ▶ Denies teachers the opportunity to cocreate safe spaces for students ▶ Promotes shame and silence instead of encouraging transparency and trust ▶ Dismisses the systemic inequities that lead to unequal access to resources ▶ Undermines the humanity of students ▶ Demonstrates that students will not be supported outside of learning ▶ Encourages secrecy in regards to what is really bothering the student
"Why did your mother drop you off so late?"	▶ Blames students for what is not within their control ▶ Welcomes students with hostility rather than care

(continues)

(continued)

OUR STATEMENTS EXPLAINED	OUR IMPACT
"I can't see you. Why isn't your camera on?"	▶ Relegates engagement to one measure of virtual presence, depriving students of the ability to participate in different ways ▶ Disregards the trauma students may experience when seeing themselves on camera (Pat-Horenczyk and Brom 2007) ▶ Disallows the opportunity for students to express why their cameras are off ▶ Does not consider the mental, social, and emotional toll of students being called out in front of their classmates ▶ Polices student's bodies while at home ▶ Robs students of the ability to learn comfortably while at home
"This curriculum is not for 'these' kids." "These kids are traumatized and failing no matter what I do." "These kids don't want to learn." "These kids can't pronounce certain words, and they don't even know what they mean."	▶ Blames Black and Brown children for not adapting to a Eurocentric culture and curriculum ▶ Stigmatizes students of color who experience trauma as incapable of learning ▶ Perpetuates academic, cultural, and social trauma by focusing on students' inability to meet standards instead of on what students need holistically to achieve academically, developmentally, socially, and emotionally ▶ Fails to acknowledge the various learning needs of the students ▶ Uses curriculum as a pipeline instead of as a wire that can be bent to spark students' critical consciousness

your cameras on!" or "No eating during class" and used other body- and home-controlling statements while teaching remotely. We had little to no idea what our students were going through or what their families were going through. In our quest for engagement and some sort of school structure, we were disregarding possible trauma responses and policing students' bodily autonomy as they sat in their own homes. Teaching is evolving into a practice with therapeutic accents, and this can be challenging for those of us with little resources and training in trauma-responsive pedagogy. Although our intentions may be pure, our actions and words have a lasting impact on our students. They will often forget our lessons, our metaphors, and our instructions but they will often remember how we honored their dignity and held space for their inherent worth no matter what they were experiencing. To stop unconsciously punishing our students for their trauma responses while simultaneously retraumatizing them, we need to become conscious of all the ways we may dismiss, ignore, and push their trauma to the margins with the intention to teach them, thus dismissing their humanity.

> *Teaching is evolving into a practice with therapeutic accents.*

SCENES FROM A CLASSROOM
Social Media and Crowdsourced Teacher Activities

"Put Your Problems in This Paper Bag!"

You google a topic like "socioemotional learning" (or "social-emotional learning") and find a teaching activity that feels fun and imaginative. Or, while scrolling through social media, a cute idea that has gone viral jumps out at you and you think, "I want to try that." You don't have the larger schema around socioemotional learning, but it feels OK. After all, it is just one activity. You decide to bring it to your morning meeting so that students can start the day by tucking their problems away. "Here's a bag. Each of you can take a sticky note and write down a problem that you're having." Next, you invite children to share their problems out loud with the class. Children share problems they are experiencing at home, with their self-esteem, and with their community. You then say, "Thank you for sharing. Now, we are going to put these problems in a bag, tie the bag up, and leave it at the door so we can focus on what really matters here: learning."

Here's what you risk: Isolating children who are in pain. Conducting a vulnerable session without creating a safe space for children to support each other throughout the day. Inviting children to open up wounds that you do not have the tools or intentions to heal. Teaching children to dissociate and compartmentalize their circumstances and emotions instead of inviting their full humanity into the classroom.

Teaching Character and Values Education, Mindfulness, and Social-Emotional Learning in Silos

You just received another social-emotional curriculum and you've been mandated to teach it at the beginning of the day. It includes mindfulness practices and activities for understanding emotions and for building relationships. You begin the day asking students how they feel, you invite them to take deep breaths, and you even study various feelings with them. You take the work a step further by helping students to understand the school values and lead them through various activities that help them to practice the values. Where love is a value, you invite them to do a greeting sharing what they love about a teammate. However, when you transition to other content areas, none of the character, values, and social-emotional work that you've done with students transfers. Instead, they are invited to buckle down, to do their work, and stay focused.

Here's what you risk: When we teach social-emotional learning, character, and values education outside of our academic content areas, our teaching is packaged in compartmentalized ways and the integration with academic content is missing. In this compartmentalized way, we see how academic experiences are out of touch with the lived realities of students (Simmons 2021) and how they will have to navigate the traumas they face and have inherited. Worse, when doing this work under the guise of mindfulness, we run the risk of weaponizing a practice that is inherently meant to heal (Duane et al. 2022). Our speech will not match our behavior because we will tell them to push through while ignoring how their trauma responses could be a profound gateway for the cultivation of their inner life. We will risk seeing a decrease in students' authentic participation. We send the message that creating healing-centered classroom spaces for the whole child isn't our work. There's an absence of trauma-responsive pedagogy. Teaching all these programs without equity and social justice in mind is harmful.

Going Beyond Your School's Mission, Vision, Values, and Benchmarks to Grow

Many schools have a mission, a vision, and values that inform their climate, culture, and curriculum. The mission drives the purpose and pedagogy; the vision illustrates the desired impact that the mission will ultimately have on the community that is being served; and the values delineate the beliefs that shape how students are educated. At my school in New Orleans, we envisioned giving our students a progressive and rigorous education in every content area so that they could meet the college- and career-readiness standards of their grade level and ultimately end generational poverty by going to college. However, this was *our* mission as a school, and these were our values *for* our students. We did not include their voices in this mission and vision, and their families didn't have a say either. Although our approach was well intentioned, it was dismissive at best and educational colonization at worst. In her book *Teaching Community*, bell hooks encourages educators "to work to find ways to teach and share knowledge in a manner that does not reinforce existing structures of domination" (2003). We never asked students what they wanted to learn, who they wanted to be, and what they would have to navigate and manage in their own lives to realize the full expression of themselves. We simply told them where they were going and insisted on how they should get there. We entered a community with the unconscious effort to colonize our students, their families, and their community at large by telling them which values they should adopt and aspire toward and how. In addition, our lofty goals did not connect with the classroom management strategies I learned or the academic achievement goals I had to uphold.

I didn't learn how to support children who were experiencing trauma in my teacher training. I know I'm not alone in this—few programs include units on trauma-informed education. When a student cursed, threw furniture during fits, tore the classroom apart in frustration, and smeared bodily fluids on the walls, I didn't always think, *This is a trauma response and trauma responses are a way students communicate their pain.* Unfortunately, there weren't many institutional solutions outside of writing referrals, sending children to the office or a take-a-break corner, and implementing positive behavioral interventions and supports. In addition to referrals, seeking the support of the school social worker, reaching out to family members, and exercising my duty as a mandated reporter, I decided to do what many teachers do: implement what we had. I didn't want to send the message that I couldn't handle my students by sending them to the principal's office for every single disruption. Back then, I was not thinking about who a student would be twenty years from now, how they would remember me, and why it was important to help them be more of their best selves. I didn't wonder how a student would transmute the cards they were dealt. Instead, I solely focused on how to get them to reach a benchmark, how to close the so called achievement gap between them and more affluent peers (Milner 2012), and how to help them succeed academically. I quickly learned this had to change.

> I didn't learn how to support children who were experiencing trauma in my teacher training. I know I'm not alone in this.

At that time, I was doing the best I could with what I had. As I grew, so did the chapters of my teaching narrative. Yours will grow, too.

SECTION **2**

WHY ● NOT?

Trauma-Responsive Classrooms Promote the Well-Being of All Students

COURTNEY N. BAKER

As Arlène's examples in Section 1 suggest, educators are uniquely poised not only to support students who have experienced trauma but also to prevent students from experiencing trauma at school. Trauma-responsive schools use an integrated set of research-informed practices intended to achieve these goals. This section will explore the guiding principles and research supporting trauma-responsive schools. I will start by reviewing the historical and theoretical contexts that shaped the trauma-responsive school movement. I write this section as a psychologist dedicated to increasing knowledge about trauma-informed approaches in schools, including understanding how and in what ways they are effective in improving the well-being of students and educators. My work is grounded in the evidence, leverages best-practices, and deeply values the lived experiences of students and educators. As such, I offer this synthesis as a jumping off point to understand and effectively implement trauma-responsive pedagogy.

Educators are uniquely poised not only to support students who have experienced trauma but also to prevent students from experiencing trauma at school.

Adverse Childhood Experiences and Trauma-Responsive Approaches

Trauma-responsive teaching is the application of trauma-informed care to education. Trauma-informed care was originally developed in human services and health care settings and describes systems that understand the prevalence and impact of trauma; recognize the signs and symptoms of trauma in both the system users and the staff; and respond by changing practices, policies, and procedures to ameliorate rather than exacerbate the effects of trauma (Brown et al. 2012; Harris and Fallot 2001; Substance Abuse and Mental

Health Services Administration [SAMHSA] 2014). Trauma-informed care grew from a stakeholder movement—adults speaking out about the experiences they had as children in residential or psychiatric care, such as restraint and seclusion, institutionalization, and the disruption of their relationships with caregivers—that identified the "care" they received as harmful rather than healing.

Although it originated in mental health and substance abuse treatment settings, trauma-informed care is relevant to schools as well. Education offers a pathway for all children to gain key skills and become contributing citizens. Especially for systemically marginalized populations, education also provides a mechanism for society to move toward social justice (Gilliam 2016; Holliday et al. 2014). Though the potential is enormous, the education system has also historically failed students. Examples include disproportional instances of exclusionary discipline and special education, bullying by students and teachers, restraint and seclusion of students with disabilities, and the control of bodies—especially Black bodies—apparent in both historical and present-day educational reform.

The Significance of Adverse Childhood Experiences (ACEs)

Around the same time that trauma-informed care was gaining traction in mental health and substance abuse settings, the landmark Adverse Childhood Experiences (ACEs) study was published (Centers for Disease Control and Prevention [CDC] 2010; Felitti et al. 1998). ACEs are a group of stressors that, when experienced before the age of eighteen, are linked with an increased risk of a host of negative outcomes across the life span. The measure specifically evaluated individuals' experience of psychological, physical, and sexual abuse, as well as their experiences of substance abuse, mental illness, interpersonal violence, and incarceration in their households. Subsequent expansions of the original ACEs list have included the additions of physical and emotional neglect and separation from a caregiver including by divorce, as

For more types of trauma, see Figure 3–5, pp 76–78

well as community-level adversity such as witnessing violence, experiencing discrimination, feeling unsafe in one's neighborhood, being bullied, and living in foster care (CDC 2010; Cronholm et al. 2015). Because the original ACEs study was conducted with people attending their routine health care screening visits, the researchers also had access to a variety of health indicators, including, for example, smoking, obesity, depressed mood, suicide attempts, alcoholism, drug use, and unsafe sexual behavior. If you are interested in knowing your own ACEs score, you can complete the quiz in the online article by Starecheski (2015).

The ACEs study and its subsequent replications are associated with several important take-home points (CDC 2010; Felitti et al. 1998; Merrick et al. 2018). First, ACEs are common, with more than half of participants experiencing one or more ACE. Readers of the original ACEs study were stunned, having assumed that very few individuals in the general population would have experienced any of these toxic stressors while growing up, and even fewer would have experienced several. Although the original report was shocking enough, researchers now know that the prevalence of ACEs is even higher than originally reported. The reason is that the original data came from a large sample of mostly white, insured, high school- and college-educated, mostly middle-class adults. Research since the original ACEs study found that some populations are at an even greater risk of experiencing ACEs. For example, women; individuals from low-income, racial and ethnic minority, and urban backgrounds; and people already involved with mental health, substance abuse, or child welfare systems are more likely to experience ACEs and also tend to experience multiple ACEs (Alim et al. 2006; Garcia et al. 2017; Merrick et al. 2018). The ongoing impacts of the coronavirus pandemic will be experienced by many people, especially members of marginalized populations, as additional ACEs (Baker et al. 2021; Golberstein et al. 2020).

Women; individuals from low-income, racial and ethnic minority, and urban backgrounds; and people already involved with mental health, substance abuse, or child welfare systems are more likely to experience ACEs and also tend to experience multiple ACEs.

The second main takeaway of the ACEs study was that the more ACEs people experience, the more likely they are to also have a host of poor health outcomes, including, for example, depression, heart disease, and obesity (CDC 2010; Felitti et al. 1998; Merrick et al. 2018). The pattern is similar for health-risk behaviors, such as smoking, and well-being outcomes, like unemployment and not graduating from high school. In fact, researchers have documented a consistent, graded, upward-sloping relationship, such that each additional ACE an individual has increases their odds of experiencing any number of poor outcomes across the life span (see Figure 2–1).

The same concerning pattern exists between ACEs and educational outcomes (Overstreet and Mathews 2011; Rossen 2020). In general, children with more ACEs perform less well academically and cognitively, are less engaged with and connected to school, and are more likely to be retained, placed in special education, truant, suspended and to drop out (Perfect et al. 2016; Porche et al. 2011, 2016). As one example of the relationship

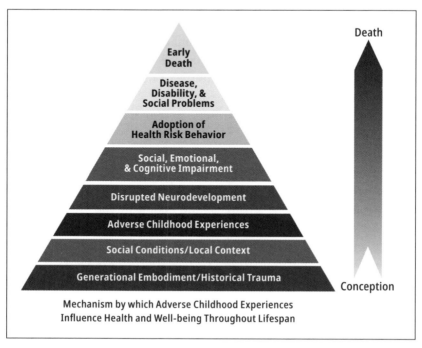

FIGURE 2–1 *The ACE Pyramid (CDC)*

between ACEs and school outcomes, researchers documented that each additional ACE elementary school students had increased their odds of academic failure, attendance problems, and school behavior problems (Blodgett and Lanigan 2018). In another study, this one with low-income, urban youth, only 3 percent of students who experienced zero ACEs had a learning or behavior problem, in contrast to 50 percent of the students who had four or more ACEs (Burke et al. 2011).

The third and final main point from the ACEs study is that the impacts of ACEs add up over time (CDC 2010; Merrick et al. 2018). In contrast to what are sometimes referred to as "big T" traumas, in which one's life is threatened (or, for a child, a caregiver's life is threatened or lost), ACEs do not typically result in acute traumatic stress responses such as posttraumatic stress disorder (PTSD). Instead, ACEs negatively impact the developing brains and bodies of children by, for example, chronically activating their fight-or-flight responses. In the short term, this is an adaptive way to survive the situation. However, this hypervigilance to threat makes learning and growth—key outcomes educators hope to foster in classrooms—difficult. When left unaddressed, the ACEs that individuals experience as children compound over time, laying a foundation of social, emotional, behavioral, and cognitive impairment upon which larger and more significant health and social problems are built.

Burnout and Secondary Traumatic Stress

Of course, educators are people, too, who may also have experienced ACEs growing up and might find it challenging to remain calm, self-regulate, and manage challenges in the classroom when they are, themselves, in fight-or-flight mode. Teaching under normal conditions is a stressful job (Montgomery and Rupp 2005). Combined with a lack of support and resources, chronic stress at work can result in burnout, which is characterized by feelings of emotional exhaustion, detachment, and inefficacy (Maslach, Schaufeli, and Leiter 2001). Secondary traumatic stress results from vicariously

To see examples of how students may be traumatized at school, see Figure 1–2, pp 13–14 experiencing traumatic events, typically through communications with students, and is characterized by PTSD-like symptoms such as hypervigilance, nightmares, and avoidance of the people or places associated with the trauma (Stamm 2009). Educators can experience either or both of these syndromes.

A simple but useful metaphor is to imagine that everyone has a "cup." That cup is refilled by things that bring health, connectedness, joy, accomplishment, and meaning. Julie Morgenstern uses the acronym SELF as a way to remember how to fill those cups, and it stands for Sleep and rest; Exercise and eating well; Love and relationships with family, friends, and community; and Fun and leisure. A sense of mastery and achievement, in work or non-work activities, also fills cups. Lastly, doing the rewarding but difficult work of contemplating and making sense of relationships, work, life, and legacy is the final way to fill cups. There is even a construct that sits in opposition to the burnout and secondary traumatic stress experienced by educators and other helping professionals called compassion satisfaction, which is defined as the pleasure and satisfaction one gets from helping others.

Research shows that "filling cups" can be done in small doses throughout the day, and that it can be done in as few as two hours per day (Sharif et al. 2021), although the sweet spot is between two and five hours per day. Cups are naturally emptied when people work hard to reach goals, give to others, and contribute meaningfully to their communities. The problem is not that cups are filled and emptied on a daily basis, but rather that individuals encounter situations and stressors that tax their ability to cope, tipping the balance over time toward an emptier and emptier cup. When the balance becomes extremely disrupted, people become vulnerable to syndromes like burnout and secondary traumatic stress. Recovering from these challenges often requires supports and interventions, so it is worth leveraging resources to prevent them from happening in the first place.

Teachers who experience burnout and secondary traumatic stress are less effective, experience more disruptive behavior in the classroom, have worse student–teacher relationships, have students who are more stressed and show less academic achievement, and are more likely to leave the profession (Herman et al. 2018; Hoglund et al. 2015; Oberle and Schonert-Reichl 2016). Trauma-responsive schools maximize teachers' protective factors and minimize their stressors, so that teachers can cope effectively, avoid burnout and secondary traumatic stress, teach and support their students, and stay engaged in the teaching profession. If you are interested in learning more about your own level of burnout and secondary traumatic stress, see Stamm (2009–2012).

As an example, which I will return to at the close of this section, a child with a chronically activated stress response may struggle to stay calm and productive in the face of a routine classroom interaction. A teacher who may also lack effective self-regulation in the face of stress may more quickly escalate the situation than is necessary. The following scene may play out:

> **TEACHER:** Everyone write the answers to problems 1 through 5 on your papers.
>
> **STUDENT:** [off-task]
>
> **TEACHER:** [child name], please face forward and focus on your work!
>
> **STUDENT:** [tears paper up and throws it on the ground]
>
> **TEACHER:** I'm sending you out since you can't meet classroom expectations. Go to the office.
>
> **STUDENT:** [leaves the classroom, misses out on the opportunity to learn, and likely engages in punitive interactions with other educators in the main office]

Trauma-informed care, including its application to education, grew out of an awareness that everyone can be adversely affected by ACEs. The model is a universal or population-level model, meaning that the prevalence and impact of ACEs is so clear from the literature that it is reasonable to assume that systems, including schools, need to adapt to this reality. Educators do not need to know the specific ACEs score of an individual, though they may be able to surmise it by knowing about the person's history, and they may be able to use it to explain behavior that is otherwise confusing such as emotional dysregulation in

Everyone can be adversely affected by ACEs.

the context of relationship transitions like goodbyes. In addition, though ACEs are important, they are only one element in the complexity of the human experience, and they do not dictate the future. The goal instead is to adopt an approach—trauma-responsive teaching, in this case—that supports everyone in the classroom who may have experienced trauma while also preventing students and educators from experiencing any additional toxic stressors while at school.

Balancing Risk with Resilience Across Development and Context

The ACEs studies have focused on adversity, but humans are complex, change with time, and exist within multiple spheres of influence that each contribute elements of risk and resilience. Resilience is defined as the ability to face challenges successfully and bounce back from stressors. Resiliencies are diverse and span the biological (i.e., genetic predisposition against developing a mental illness, adaptable temperament or personality, physical health), psychological (i.e., self-regulation ability, coping skills, the ability to cognitively reframe negative or distorted thoughts), and social (i.e., supportive family or social network, high-quality schools, systems that prevent discrimination). Two theoretical perspectives help us understand the interplay of risk and resilience, specifically providing guidance on how to reduce risk and boost resilience to improve health, educational, and social outcomes: Bronfenbrenner's (1992) developmental ecological systems theory and developmental psychopathology.

Humans develop in their social context, with those social contexts that are "closest," such as the family and the classroom, being most important.

Bronfenbrenner's (1992) developmental ecological systems theory, along with subsequent iterations of the model (e.g., phenomenological variant of ecological systems theory [Spencer, Dupree, and Haretmann 1997]), posits that humans develop in their social context, with those social contexts that are "closest," such as the family and the classroom, being most important. Contexts that are farther away, such as the school and community, and the societal, cultural, economic, and political impacts of the region, nation, and the world, have important impacts as well. For this reason, the developmental ecological model is often depicted as a bull's-eye, with the individual at the center, surrounded by increasingly distal contexts, and with the impacts across and between contexts playing out over time (see Figure 2–2). Of course, the proximity and therefore the impact of these contexts can shift. For example, when children are at lunch and recess, school becomes their primary context rather than classroom. When they are at a Boys & Girls Club, their primary context might become community. Impacts from more distal contexts can be buffered and protected against by influences in the closer contexts.

FIGURE 2–2 *Developmental Ecological Systems Theory*

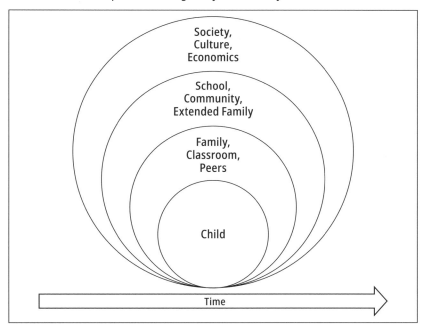

Developmental psychopathology is a perspective that explains how individuals develop problems such as psychological disorders over time (Achenbach 2015; Cicchetti 1984). Developmental psychopathology posits that genetic, individual, family, and environmental influences interact over time to either promote typical or atypical developmental outcomes. Influences that boost developmental trajectories are called protective factors and may

When protective factors are maximized and risk factors are minimized, individuals are most likely to achieve their optimal, healthy developmental trajectory.

include, for example, effective coping skills, reading to young children at home, and access to high-quality schools. Influences that dampen developmental trajectories over time are called risk factors and may include, for example, ACEs, poverty, and racism. Everyone experiences both strengths and weaknesses. However, due to systematic injustice within the United States, specific sociodemographic characteristics like race, ethnicity, socioeconomic status, religion, and immigration status correlate with the likelihood of experiencing specific risk factors (Crenshaw 2017). When protective factors are maximized and risk factors are minimized, individuals are most likely to achieve their optimal, healthy developmental trajectory (see Figure 2–3).

FIGURE 2–3 *Developmental Psychopathology (Adapted from Halfon et al. [2014])*

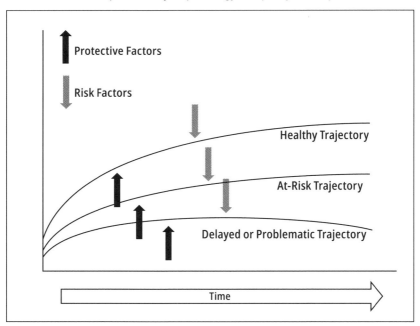

For example, a fifth-grader may live in an unsafe neighborhood, witness community violence, and experience discrimination, all of which are ACEs and risk factors. However, the potential negative impacts of these more distal risk factors may be mitigated by an adaptable temperament, strong problem-solving skills, and positive relationships with parents and teachers. The student may also have experienced protective factors earlier in life, such as appropriate discipline practices, engaged and active parental supervision, and access to a high-quality preschool. In this scenario, though the adversity that the fifth-grader experiences may depress their developmental trajectory, the numerous supports, in turn, bolster the student's growth and success, keeping them on a path toward health and well-being.

Building Resilience

Taken together, developmental ecological systems theory (Bronfenbrenner 1992; Spencer et al. 1997) and developmental psychopathology (Achenbach 2015; Cicchetti 1984) provide guidance when translating the science of ACEs into the practice of trauma-responsive teaching. Now that I have explored the historical and theoretical contexts that shaped the trauma-responsive school movement, it is time to shift this discussion to the "how" of trauma-responsive education.

Trauma-responsive schools understand the prevalence and impact of trauma, recognize the signs and symptoms of trauma in students and school staff, and respond by changing policies, practices, and procedures to reduce the impact of past ACEs and trauma and also to prevent them in the future (Harris and Fallot 2001; Overstreet and Chafouleas 2016; SAMHSA 2014). Guidelines have been developed that adapt trauma-informed approaches to education to support the implementation of trauma-responsive schools (e.g., Cole et al. 2013). Trauma-responsive education is implemented at the school or district level, and its components typically include leadership consultation, professional development training about trauma, teacher skill-building and coaching, and evidence-based interventions for students with clinical stress reactions or psychological distress. Depending on the model, each of these pillars of trauma-responsive education can be implemented in-house or through partnerships with the community. Though the empirical literature on trauma-responsive schools is new, studies have found that when a school adopts trauma-informed approaches, staff knowledge of the effects of trauma increases, staff attitudes become more trauma informed, and there are fewer

When a school adopts trauma-informed approaches, staff knowledge of the effects of trauma increases, staff attitudes become more trauma informed, and there are fewer suspensions, expulsions, and student behavior issues.

suspensions, expulsions, and student behavior issues (Dorado et al. 2016; McIntyre et al. 2019; von der Embse et al. 2018).

Though trauma-responsive education must occur at the system level to be fully effective, one of the biggest challenges for teachers is translating what they learn in foundational professional development trainings about ACEs and trauma into their classrooms. In fact, I know from my own research that two key facilitators of the successful implementation of trauma-responsive education include (1) knowing what to do and (2) self-efficacy that it can be done (Wittich et al. 2020). When these are supported by adequate resources and a shared commitment to the work, educators are well equipped to tackle the challenges of implementing trauma-responsive education (Wittich et al. 2020). For this reason, I will spend the rest of this section reviewing the two main ways that teachers can implement trauma-responsive education in their classrooms: developing lagging skills and building supportive relationships (Greene and Ablon 2006; Shonkoff 2016). Each of these methods of boosting students' resilience can be integrated into the day-to-day activities of the classroom, and each plays a central role in the set of research-informed practices that together create a trauma-informed school or district, especially when educator well-being is also supported. Of course, trauma-responsive classrooms must also minimize risk, particularly through reducing or eliminating practices that may lead to students being traumatized at school. I will discuss this complementary element of trauma-informed classrooms at the close of this chapter.

To see examples of how students may be traumatized at school, see Figure 1–2, pp 13–14

Developing Lagging Social, Emotional, and Behavioral Skills

Child development is typically explained with a stage theory, which means that, in general, it proceeds in order, over time, and that stages typically cannot be skipped. The stages are predictably pinned to children's ages, such that it is reasonable to expect a seven-year-old to possess the skills typical of that age. Educators tend to understand typical child development well. They usually took at least one child development course as part of their training, and they frequently employ age-normed screenings as part of their routine benchmarking or special education processes at school. They are experts not only at understanding certain areas of child development relevant to learning, such as reading or math skills, but also at using scaffolding within the zone of proximal development (Vygotsky et al. 1994) to help children continue to grow those skills. Finally, educators work with large numbers of children across their careers, and they watch those children develop skills over the course of the academic year, a process that is particularly notable for educators teaching students in early childhood and during puberty. Taken together, educators tend to have fairly reliable "internal norms" for typical child development milestones.

However, there are a few important take-home points about child development that are critical to understand for teachers interested in trauma-responsive teaching. First, students may have lagging skills or skills that are developmentally younger than their chronological age. There are many reasons why this might occur, including having experienced ACEs and trauma (Greene and Ablon 2006). Though the full chronicling of what lagging skills might look like in comparison to typical development is beyond the scope of this book, with regard to social, emotional, and behavioral skills, these children typically look immature. Greene and Ablon (2006) catalog that, in comparison to their peers, they:

- seem less able to cope with routine peer interactions or classroom expectations;
- have poorer impulse control, ability to delay gratification, and executive functioning skills;
- experience poorer emotion regulation and more frequent or intense uncomfortable feelings, including worry, anger, sadness, guilt, and shame;
- appear more vigilant or fearful, like they expect bad things to happen;

■ are cognitively inflexible, with particular challenges with changes to routines, ambiguity, transitions, abstract concepts, and perspective taking;

■ have lower self-esteem, less initiative or persistence, and more challenges forming a positive identity; and

■ struggle with relationships stemming from challenges with attachment and/or social skills (see also "Building Supportive Relationships" later in this chapter).

Children need to learn these skills, and in chronological order, so that their developmental age can catch up to their chronological age. For example, if a student is seven years old, but their math skill is comparable to that of a five-year-old, then math instruction must generally begin at the five-year-old level and proceed forward, in order. This is not surprising to educators. However, sub in the word *social* or *emotional* skill instead of math skill, and educators have a harder time imagining that they might need to scaffold developmentally appropriate learning of the social or emotional skills of a five-year-old in their classrooms of seven-year-olds. In the context of the many stressors of the classroom, educators can even make the mistake of seeing the child with lagging skills as misbehaving intentionally, being manipulative, or not trying hard enough.

Second, children's development includes many facets, such as physical, cognitive, social, and emotional development. Though development typically proceeds through stages in order, a child's developmental profile may be "rugged," meaning that the student can have average or above-average verbal and motor skills but still have lagging social or emotional skills. It is critically important that educators approach each child from a lens of that child's strengths, resisting defining the child only by areas in which there is a need for developmental acceleration. Unfortunately, education reform has pushed classroom education for early grades toward a model more appropriate for more advanced developmental levels, such as requiring kindergarteners to sit still at desks for long periods of time and take standardized tests without interacting with peers or teachers. Even when teachers are aware of the developmental mismatch in their classrooms, it can sometimes be a challenge to push back against school, district, or policy requirements that are developmentally inappropriate.

    Third, children who are physically larger for their age are perceived as more mature, and Black boys, in particular, are overly noticed for and misperceived as hostile and misbehaving when those behaviors are either minor or normative (Giordano et al. 2020). Teachers have been shown to hold higher academic expectations for White students in comparison with Black and Latinx students (Tenenbaum and Ruck 2007). At times, the pendulum can swing even farther—not only are the adults less likely to provide supports to Black and brown students, but they are also more likely to engage in negative talk or harsh interactions. Additionally, teachers are more likely to underestimate the academic abilities of children with lagging developmental skills related to both social skills and attention—arguably the children who need the most care and attention—and those lowered expectations are linked with less academic growth over the school year (Baker et al. 2015). If a student is perceived as more mature or more threatening because of their size or skin color, adults may be less likely to provide the scaffolding they need to cope with and learn from the situation. In each of these contexts, not only will the student struggle to learn the lagging skill, but it will also be an unrewarding and challenging situation for everyone involved.

    Adults tend to notice lagging skills when behaviors are more disruptive. For example, children with lagging skills who are quiet and more withdrawn (often girls), as opposed to throwing tables, can go unnoticed. Without universal screening (the equivalent of benchmarking for social and emotional skills), these students can slip through the cracks. (Pickford et al. 2021). If adults don't notice their lagging skills these children are less likely to be referred to the special education evaluation process or to external resources and are therefore less likely to get early and effective support.

> *It is critically important that educators approach each child from a lens of that child's strengths, resisting defining the child only by areas in which there is a need for developmental acceleration.*

Over- and undernoticing are two sides of the same automatic human cognitive process, which takes these particular forms due to the current norms of society. Every human being possesses implicit social attitudes, so it is not possible to "erase" them; rather, the goal is to become aware of them and work actively against their assumptions. Several evidence-based approaches to enhance equity exist, such as engaging in professional development and self-reflection about internalized bias (to take a look at your own implicit social attitudes, see Harvard [n.d.]), using normed instruments whenever possible, and disaggregating data by sociodemographic characteristic to check for patterns. Trauma-informed approaches also enhance equity by training educators to ask themselves questions about a student's behavior—such as "What might have happened to this student?" or "How might this behavior serve an adaptive purpose for this student?"—before reacting to it with, for example, punitive or exclusionary discipline.

Trauma-informed approaches also enhance equity by training educators to ask themselves questions about a student's behavior—such as "What might have happened to this student?" or "How might this behavior serve an adaptive purpose for this student?"—before reacting to it with, for example, punitive or exclusionary discipline.

The final take-home point related to child development is that all humans need to learn social, emotional, and behavioral skills just like they learn math or reading skills. Humans are lucky in that they essentially do not have a critical period or a point at which teaching a new skill becomes impossible. It is almost never too late for humans to develop their lagging skills, though earlier intervention has the ability to impact the child's developmental trajectory in a more significant way. Nonetheless, teachers often feel underequipped to handle these types of issues in the classroom, in part because their preservice and inservice training typically does not focus on it.

I deeply believe, however, that teachers are actually the perfect individuals to tackle this challenge of developing lagging skills. Teachers know better than anyone else how to teach a skill. With the right tools and a shift in their mindsets, they can apply that depth of knowledge to the teaching of social, emotional, and behavioral skills. Just like teaching academic skills, the process is simple: provide explicit instruction, model, practice, coach, and reward the use of the skills. Like all skills, consistent practice is the best way to learn them. For example, skills related to following teacher instructions or coping with stress by deep breathing can be directly taught in groups or individually, modeled by the teacher, practiced routinely in the classroom until mastery is achieved, coached if additional supports are needed, and rewarded using tangible (e.g., a sticker chart) or relationship-focused (e.g., praise) ways, all in a consistent manner over time.

Teachers are actually the perfect individuals to tackle this challenge of developing lagging skills. Teachers know better than anyone else how to teach a skill.

Teachers do not need to worry that they are the only ones responsible for identifying and developing lagging social, emotional, and behavior skills. The data-gathering, problem-solving, and tiered intervention approaches of multitiered systems of support (MTSS) can be applied to social, emotional, and behavioral skills in the same way, which can help teachers when the challenge is too pervasive or significant to tackle in the classroom alone (Briesch et al. 2020). As a reminder, MTSS is a widely utilized framework to enhance the adoption and implementation of evidence-informed practices in schools. MTSS was developed out of Response to Intervention and was first applied to student academic outcomes. In the last decade, the model has been expanded to include social, emotional, and behavioral outcomes. For example, the use of screening and assessment, universal (tier 1) programs, targeted prevention (tier 2) and intervention (tier 3) programs for students who need them, and integration with other in-school and community resources can support children with significantly lagging skills related to untreated trauma or other clinically significant psychological distress (Chafouleas et al. 2016). Because teachers are most likely to be involved in this work at the universal level, the following subsections describe two tier 1 approaches that embody trauma-responsive teaching: safe, predictable, and supportive classrooms and social-emotional learning programs.

Safe, Predictable, and Supportive Classrooms

Teachers can use several strategies to create a safe and predictable classroom environment that is developmentally appropriate and emotionally supportive and that utilizes positive discipline strategies. Such an environment will help all students learn, but it is especially critical for students with a history of trauma or ACEs who are hypervigilant to threats in their environments. Some key strategies include developing clear class rules, learning how to give effective commands, establishing routines for attention and transitions, adopting a four-to-one positive-to-negative interaction ratio, learning how to give behavior-specific praise and (if needed) tangible rewards, using planned ignoring, learning how to give concise and informative reprimands, and practicing (if needed) how to properly implement brief time-outs that do not take away from instructional time (Simonsen et al. 2008). A key distinction here is that creating a safe, predictable, and supportive classroom provides developmentally appropriate environmental supports that help students regulate their own emotions and behavior. Punitive and exclusionary discipline, which is reactive, harsh, and typically associated with loss of instructional time, attempts to control students behavior and sometimes bodies, and, if that fails, eliminate students and their behavior from the classroom altogether.

For more trauma-responsive strategies, see "How Can I Weave Trauma-Responsive Education into the Fabric of My Teaching?" pp 68–89

Safe, predictable, supportive classrooms with appropriate, engaging instruction can reduce disruptive behavior and increase social skills, emotion regulation, and academic achievement (Simonsen et al. 2008). Use of these strategies also protects against the snap judgments, sometimes driven by implicit social attitudes, that can drive the use of disproportionate punitive and exclusionary discipline (Gregory et al. 2016). Creating safe, predictable, and supportive classrooms is a skill set that teachers develop and hone, just like any other skill. At the same time, most teachers entering the profession are underprepared in this area (Begeny and Martens 2006). Although diving into the details of these strategies is beyond the scope of this work, you may learn more about it in *No More Taking Away Recess and Other Problematic Discipline Practices* (2013) by Gianna Cassetta and Brook Sawyer, another book in this series.

Social-Emotional Learning Programs

Social-emotional learning is an umbrella term for the processes that lead to appropriately managing emotions, setting and achieving goals, having empathy for others, establishing and maintaining relationships, and making responsible choices (Durlak et al. 2007). Effective social-emotional learning typically includes several core skills pitched to the appropriate developmental level, such as feelings identification and vocabulary, managing strong feelings (deep breathing, take a break, coping self-talk), identifying feelings in others, being a good friend, and problem-solving (Joseph and Strain 2003; Lawson et al. 2019; see also Collaborative for Academic, Social, and Emotional Learning n.d.). Social-emotional learning programs are typically curricula that teachers can incorporate into the school day, which come prepackaged with teacher manuals, supplementary materials, and homework. Many effective social-emotional learning programs exist on the market, such as Second Step, Promoting Alternative Thinking Strategies (PATHS), and Incredible Years Dinosaur School, among others (Domitrovich et al. 2007; Upshur et al. 2019; Webster-Stratton et al. 2004; Webster-Stratton et al. 2008). The evidence for certain (though not all) social-emotional learning programs is robust and suggests that they can prevent behavior problems and emotional distress while also promoting prosocial behavior and academic achievement over the long term (Durlak et al. 2011; Jones et al. 2015; McClelland et al. 2017).

Classroom behavior management strategies, which are teacher focused and lay the foundation for children to observe, practice, and grow lagging skills, and social-emotional learning programs, which are child focused and provide explicit instruction in developing lagging skills, share the same end goal: building resilience. Specifically, through explicit instruction, modeling, practice, coaching, and reinforcement, these strategies can help children develop the social competence and emotion regulation skills that underpin academic achievement. These approaches are two key tools that can be used by teachers, in tandem with their preexisting skill sets, to train lagging social, emotional, and behavioral skills in students, including in those who have experienced ACEs or trauma.

Building Supportive Relationships

The other way that teachers can implement trauma-responsive education in their classrooms, in addition to developing lagging skills, is building supportive relationships with students (Shonkoff 2016). Effective instruction, including developing lagging skills, rests upon the foundation of the student–teacher relationship. It can feel frustrating or tangential to spend time on relationship building, especially when the pressures to focus on academic goals or immediately address students' lagging skills in the form of disruptive behavior are intense (Howard et al. 2020). Luckily, most educators enjoy working with students, value their perspectives, and have dedicated their lives to lifting up students' dreams and goals. Even brand-new educators have typically worked with dozens of children, so they also have experience interacting with young people in developmentally appropriate ways. Taken together, educators are well equipped to do the work of developing safe, predictable, and supportive relationships with all their students, even those who are harder to reach.

The research tells us that positive relationships are an important foundation for learning and student well-being (see Figure 2–4).

FIGURE 2–4 *Impacts of Student–Teacher Relationships*

- Empathy, warmth, and genuineness are strongly positively related to key cognitive and emotional/behavioral student outcomes, including engagement, executive functioning, and academic achievement (Cornelius-White 2007; Roorda et al. 2011; Vandenbroucke et al. 2018).

- Early relationships may have even more power, compounding in either good or bad ways over time (Roorda et al. 2011; Vandenbroucke et al. 2018).

- Cultural congruence can be powerful. For example, in classrooms where low-income, Black students are taught by Black teachers, relationships that balance high expectations with high levels of support may lead to fewer disciplinary referrals, increased academic growth, and more prosocial behavior (Bondy and Ross 2008; Sandilos et al. 2017).

(continues)

- Cultural competence is important. In cross-cultural relationships, teachers must work to develop their awareness, knowledge, and skills related to the cultural backgrounds of their students for those relationships to be successful (Sue 2001).

- Positive student–teacher relationships can protect against other risk factors such as poverty (Silva et al. 2011) and even compensate for the negative impacts of unmet attachment needs (Hamre and Pianta 2005).

Because babies are helpless when they are born, humans evolved to develop a deep and intense emotional bond with their caregivers when they are very young. The patterns of caring, closeness, security, and responsiveness set early in a child's life by their interactions with their caregivers lay the foundation for their lifelong sense of connectedness, safety, trust, and beliefs about the self, especially in the context of relationships with others. The theory that explains this phenomenon is called attachment theory (Bowlby 1979).

Empathy, warmth, and genuineness are strongly positively related to key cognitive and emotional/behavioral student outcomes, including engagement, executive functioning, and academic achievement.

Unfortunately, many students who have experienced toxic stress or trauma have learned through personal experience that adults cannot be trusted and that relationships and closeness can lead to hurt and loss. They may have developed powerful beliefs that they are worthless and un-lovable; that other people and the world around them are unsafe, unpredictable, untrustworthy; and that their future is shortened, bleak, out of their control, or impossible to envision (Beck 2002). Attachment theory helps us understand why students take what they have internalized from previous interactions with others, including previous teachers, and attempt to replicate it with new adults. What this looks like can vary between students or even within students over time, but it almost always feels uncomfortable or challenging when you, as the teacher, are the new adult in the student's life.

It is useful to think about these patterns of behavior as stress responses evoked by the possibility or threat of a new relationship. Trauma-responsive approaches conceptualize these patterns of behavior as adaptations that the student has made to keep themselves safe and whole in the context of adversity, toxic stress, trauma, and unmet attachment needs. Arlène listed some scenarios teachers might encounter with students in Figure 1–1.

Fortunately, equally innate to humans as the attachment system is humankind's ability to learn and grow (Skinner 1965). Unsurprisingly, because humans are primed to create and thrive in relationships, the best environment to relearn how to be in relationships with others is, in fact, safe, predictable, and supportive relationships with others. As hard as the work can be, it is up to the teacher and the other adults in the student's life to take the lead and, if needed, be waiting and ready for when the student is ready to connect. Indeed, looking back over the weeks or months of hard work and observing that your relationship with a student has moved from conflict to ease or from disengagement to engagement is one of the greatest joys of teaching.

As hard as the work can be, it is up to the teacher and the other adults in the student's life to take the lead and, if needed, be waiting and ready for when the student is ready to connect.

Research has helped to identify practices to build and enhance positive student–teacher relationships. Key proactive and direct practices identified by Kincade and colleagues (2020) include

- praise and positive interactions;
- getting to know students better as individuals, including one-on-one time and student-led activities;
- validating emotions, using supportive listening, and checking in; and
- communicating care, respect, and that the student is valued.

Other methods have also been shown to support positive student–teacher relationships, such as creating safe, predictable, and supportive classrooms and teaching social-emotional learning skills (see "Developing Lagging Social, Emotional, and Behavioral Skills") as well as repairing the student–teacher relationship after conflict such as through restorative conversations (Gregory et al. 2016; see Ferlazzo [2020] for additional guidance on having restorative conversations). These strategies boil down to hundreds of subtle and explicit interactions every day that communicate safety, care, belongingness, and value to the student (Howard et al. 2020). A four-minute video called "Every Opportunity" (Atlanta Speech School 2014) vividly demonstrates the incredible power that educators have in every minute of every school day to either build up or tear down their relationships with students. For more on building safe, predictable, and supportive student–teacher relationships, as well as student–student and teacher–family relationships, see *No More Teaching Without Positive Relationships* (2020) by Jaleel R. Howard, Tanya Milner-McCall, and Tyrone C. Howard, another book in this series.

Within a trauma-responsive framework, the process by which the student–teacher relationship can retrain students who have experienced trauma and who have unmet attachment needs occurs in three ways, which can be used throughout the school day (see Figure 2–5).

FIGURE 2–5 *Safe and Supportive Relationships Help Retrain Students (Safe Schools NOLA. 2019.)*

STRATEGY	WHEN TO USE IT	WHAT IT DOES
Engage in co-regulation (i.e., calm, supportive scaffolding to help the student use their own emotion regulation skills)	When the student is distressed	Calms the stress response, retrains the brain and body, and develops emotion regulation skills
Model emotion regulation	When the teacher is distressed	Shows students how adults effectively handle big feelings
Directly teach skills and create environments related to calming the stress response, building emotion regulation skills, and facilitating safe relationships with peers and adults	Before anyone is distressed (preventative)	Builds lagging skills so that students are able to engage in school and learn (see "Developing Lagging Social, Emotional, and Behavioral Skills")

Attending to Educator Well-Being

Although the previous section made it clear that building safe, predictable, and supportive student–teacher relationships is critical to boosting resilience, I would be remiss if I did not also discuss how challenging it can feel at times and what teachers can do to navigate that challenge. As I noted, the first truth of the student–teacher relationship is that the burden falls on the shoulders of the adult, even when this may feel unfair or unrewarding (Howard et al. 2020). At the same time, it is also true that students cannot meet educators' emotional needs (Howard et al. 2020). Teachers are humans, too, with their own relationship and attachment history. As I discussed earlier, teachers who are burned out or experience secondary traumatic stress show up to school with an "empty cup" and are less able to fill the cups of their students. It is much harder to avoid taking things personally, especially in the context of relationships, when you are exhausted, short-fused, on edge, checked out, or worn down. The third and final truth is that teaching demands the full self (Howard et al. 2020). It would not be so hard or hurt so much if educators did not care.

> *The first truth of the student–teacher relationship is that the burden falls on the shoulders of the adult.*

It is not a matter of *if* the work will affect educators but rather *when*. When you consider it this way, at least some experience of teacher stress, and possibly burnout or secondary traumatic stress as well, is inevitable in your career. Compounding this issue, many schools are ill equipped to provide the supports you need to navigate through that challenge. For example, many schools lack resources, making it a struggle every day to get the most basic elements of your job done. Others are associated with high levels of staff turnover and student mobility, which inherently trigger educators' own defensive reactions to investing in new relationships. Still others perpetuate systemic racism and oppression by attempting to control students' bodies rather than support their cognitive, emotional, and behavioral growth. Teachers in unsupportive schools may feel like boats adrift on a stormy sea, unable to dedicate scarce personal resources to the work of teaching and building resilience.

Taking these truths and their associated challenges together, it is clear that teachers must prioritize self-care. Finding ways to "fill your own cup," recover from burnout, cope effectively with experiences of secondary traumatic stress, and surround yourself with personal and professional supports is as critically important to your professional success as your other tasks as an educator. In other words, the theories covered at the beginning of this section also applied to teachers: educators must find ways in their professional lives to balance risk with resilience.

> For more about self-awareness, see "Stage 1: Know Thyself" in Section 3

Although there are numerous excellent resources to support educators trying to tackle this challenge (e.g., Herman and Reinke [2014]; von der Embse et al. [2019]), it is not sustainable for individual teachers to maintain their wellness in a broken system. Ironically, even schools committed to trauma-responsive education may struggle to support teacher well-being. For example, having too few resources and perceiving student needs as being too acute stands in the way of effective implementation of trauma-responsive teaching (Wittich et al. 2020), actually becoming another source of teacher stress and potential burnout rather than a support. Even when supervisors, coaches, and leaders realize the importance of supporting educators, they struggle to translate that knowledge into action (Baker et al. 2018). Nonetheless, with careful implementation, trauma-informed approaches prioritize the well-being of everyone in the school building, including both the educators and the students. Teachers may also opt to organize study groups (see Herman and Reinke [2014] for additional guidance) or advocate for improved work conditions with their leadership. Some examples of what a school-wide commitment to educator wellness might look like, organized by the four pillars of trauma-responsive education, are described in Figure 2–6.

> *It is key that teachers reduce or eliminate the use of punitive and exclusionary discipline, address bullying, and eradicate discrimination and microaggressions, all of which may lead to students being traumatized at school.*

FIGURE 2–6 *Supporting Educator Well-Being*

WHEN	WHAT	OUTCOME
In system-wide changes implemented by **leadership**	Implement trauma-informed approaches at the school or district level (Cole et al. 2013; SAMHSA 2014), including modifying the school environment and operations to decrease educators' stress (i.e., time-off policies) and increase their supports (i.e., providing training in relaxation, mindfulness, or cognitive coping [von der Embse et al. 2019]).	Educators feel cared for and supported by their school and district leaders, know they are part of a supportive team, and feel equipped to handle both crises and the day-to-day stressors of teaching.
During foundational **professional development** trainings	Facilitate shared learning that defines and labels burnout and secondary traumatic stress, explores the impacts of these phenomena on educators and students, and creates educator self-care plans.	Educators develop a shared language to describe their personal experiences of burnout and secondary traumatic stress and are provided a mechanism to ask their supervisors and leaders for what they need to be supported and to cope.
During **coaching** to support teacher skills and the implementation of new classroom strategies	Provide holistic coaching that supports teachers' well-being and provides a safe place to explore and grow while also assisting teachers as they practice specific new skills and strategies.	Educators thrive in a supportive and collaborative relationship that holds them accountable not only for specific trauma-responsive classroom strategies but also for self-care and well-being.
By **screening for and treating** students' clinical stress reactions or psychological distress	Identify and treat students' mental health issues that can underlie behavior and learning problems in the classroom and at school, especially for students who fail to respond to typical interventions.	Educators know that their students are receiving best-practice services provided by mental health experts, allowing them to focus on teaching and building resilience.

Minimizing Risk

Of course, together with developing resilience, trauma-responsive systems must also minimize risk. The goals of trauma-informed schools are not only to ameliorate the impacts of trauma and ACEs that students have already experienced but also to prevent future traumatic experiences. Thus, it is key that teachers reduce or eliminate the use of punitive and exclusionary discipline, address bullying, and eradicate discrimination and microaggressions, all of which may lead to students being traumatized at school. Together, these strategies of minimizing risk play a key role in the set of research-informed practices that together create trauma-informed classrooms (see Figure 2–7).

FIGURE 2–7 *Minimizing Risk*

STRATEGY	WHY IT IS HARMFUL	WHAT TO DO INSTEAD
Eliminate the use of punitive and exclusionary discipline	Office discipline referrals, suspensions, and expulsions result in out-of-class time, when children lose access to instruction and the ability to practice building resilience and are exposed to higher-risk contexts such as punitive interactions with other adults, peer groups with elevated behavioral and academic challenges, and unmonitored time at home. Restraints, such as holds, and seclusions, which isolate students, attempt to physically control students' bodies; this feels unsafe, scary, and invasive to the student.	Pull in additional supports and consider lowering expectations temporarily to keep students in the classroom, offering them the chance to learn, train lagging skills, and retrain relationship schemas. Adopt a no-restraint and no-seclusion policy in the school, and, if frequent restraint and seclusion are already occurring, obtain consultation to create environments and adult–student interactions that regulate and calm students rather than dysregulate and escalate them.

(continues)

(continued)

STRATEGY	WHY IT IS HARMFUL	WHAT TO DO INSTEAD
Address bullying	Bullying, defined as repeated acts of aggression in the context of a power differential, harms students' mental health and academic performance (Rossen and Cowan 2012).	When observing bullying behavior, respond quickly, consistently, and firmly that it is unacceptable. Advocate for the school-wide adoption of evidence-based bullying prevention strategies (Rossen and Cowan 2012).
Eradicate discrimination and microaggressions	Discrimination is the unequal treatment of people based on their perceived group membership. Microaggressions are a form of discrimination that are indirect and subtle; therefore, microaggressions can be more challenging to observe and stop. Discrimination of any type communicates that the student is not welcome and has a negative impact on well-being and achievement (National Association of School Psychologists 2019).	Personally, become aware of biases (for more, see page 36), cultivate knowledge about groups different than your own, and practice skills needed to interact competently with diverse groups (Sue 2001). In the classroom, create an environment that elevates diversity, lauds counter-stereotypical exemplars, promotes empathy, and communicates immediately and firmly that discrimination of all forms is unacceptable (National Association of School Psychologists 2019; Sue et al. 2019).

Conclusion

Think back to the dialogue from earlier in which both a student and a teacher with chronically activated stress responses struggled to stay calm and productive in the face of a routine classroom interaction. In a trauma-responsive classroom that builds resilience and minimizes risk, the scene might look different:

TEACHER: Everyone write the answers to problems 1 through 5 on your papers.

STUDENT: [off-task]

TEACHER: [privately, while others are working] I see you are wiggling. Would you like some help getting started? Or would you like to use the gesture we agreed upon and ask for a break?

STUDENT: [uses gesture] I would like a break.

TEACHER: Sure, no problem. Thanks for asking for what you need. The timer is set for five minutes in the coping corner. I'll see you back here when you hear the ding.

STUDENT: [uses coping corner to calm down and then returns to his seat, does not leave the classroom, does not miss out on the opportunity to learn, practices coping skills, and retains a strong positive relationship with teacher]

TEACHER: Thank you, [child name], for taking a break and helping your body get calm and ready to work. I'm proud of you. Now that you're ready, I'm excited to see what you can do with problem 1.

In summary, research indicates that trauma-responsive classrooms provide a pathway to bolster students' resilience by developing lagging skills in the context of safe, predictable, and supportive classrooms and social-emotional learning programs; fostering healthy student–teacher relationships; and supporting educator well-being. They simultaneously minimize students' exposure to risk by reducing or eliminating the use of punitive or exclusionary discipline and other approaches that may lead to students being traumatized at school. To best achieve this goal of boosting student resilience and reducing student risk, evidence-based trauma-responsive classroom practices are utilized by teachers within larger systems that are also implementing trauma-informed education. In the next section, Arlène will offer specific examples of these principles in practice.

SECTION **3**

BUT ● **THAT**

Teaching for Healing and Transformation: Seven Stages to Trauma-Responsive Pedagogy

ARLÈNE ELIZABETH CASIMIR

When I moved to New Orleans in 2011, my classroom was made up of children who were in the womb during Hurricane Katrina in September of 2005. But that wasn't the only storm that swept through leaving mass devastation in her wake. A beautiful yet complex cultural history, generational poverty, gentrification, mass incarceration, one of the highest murder rates in the country, and ranking forty-sixth in national K–8 education meant that the natural disaster completely destabilized an already precarious community. My students never weathered the watery doom firsthand, but the traces of it—and all of the other violent inequities they were subject to—contributed to the whirlwind of extreme and vicarious trauma they would experience.

Ancient wisdom traditions from the African diaspora and Indigenous cultures teach us that every healing journey begins with a crisis.

Ironically, this is where my own healing journey began. Ancient wisdom traditions from the African diaspora and Indigenous cultures teach us that every healing journey begins with a crisis. My students' predicament brought up a lot of my own unresolved trauma as a first-generation Haitian-American from Brooklyn, New York. Acknowledging my own story and buried pain when trying to be responsive to my students' trauma made me realize all of the inner work that I would have to do while showing up for my students outwardly. I quickly learned that our collective healing would become a parallel process. Ideally, I would do this work on my own, first . . . but no college, graduate school, or teacher education experience could have prepared me for what I was experiencing in my classroom. I didn't have the capacity to go on an "eat, pray, love" sabbatical. And I couldn't afford to quit! I had to work, and the way I was *working* was not working for me or for my students. Their trauma continued to surface and disrupt our learning targets.

I realized that the supreme target was returning to wholeness. We needed to heal in the classroom. It became necessary to respond to the trauma and to remove the barriers to their learning. As I responded to my own trauma, I felt myself healing. As I healed, I could teach them how to heal through my example.

I have spent over a decade honing my practice, research, and skills to develop a parallel process-driven framework for trauma-responsive pedagogy. My hope is that this section (and this book at large in collaboration with Courtney) is an offering of the research and wisdom that we have acquired through our various experiences and studies. I hope it can support you with this imperative work now.

> *I realized that the supreme target was returning to wholeness.*

I've learned there are seven stages to becoming trauma responsive while engaging in this process alongside students (shown in Figure 3–1). Just like healing, these stages are not linear. You may find yourself spiraling through them at different points in your journey. However, I do recommend going through the process once before revisiting and going deeper in a second round. Going through all the stages could take a quarter, a semester, a year, or even three school years when taken on a school-wide basis. Trust the process and know that you come back to each stage with more depth and complexity every time. A key principle of trauma-informed healing is to be flexible (Venet 2021). After going through the seven stages once, allow yourself to return to the specific stages that you feel drawn to, what your students need, and trust the timing of your selection. It's helpful to set yourself up for success by setting a goal for how you move through the stages. That goal could be around the time it will take to go through the process, the inner work you'd like to focus on, and who you'd like to work with on your healing journey. Remember to give yourself compassion and grace. If you don't meet the goal, go back to your goal setting, set a new goal, and try again. In this work, as an infamous Haitian proverb reminds us, "Behind

> *In this work, as an infamous Haitian proverb reminds us, "Behind mountains, there are more mountains."*

mountains, there are more mountains." This means when we feel like we've arrived, there's more work to do and more places to go to heal. I also recommend that you find someone who will affirm and support you in the process.

FIGURE 3–1 *Seven Stages to Becoming Trauma Responsive*

1. Know thyself.
2. Know thy curriculum, research, and supporting educational frameworks.
3. Bear witness.
4. Feel.
5. Grieve.
6. Initiate.
7. Heal and Transform.

The stages are a process to support educators in becoming trauma responsive. The framework is also meant to be inclusive. I have had new students and educators enter at different stages in their classroom or school community. However, I know the stages work best when anyone who enters later has the opportunity to repeat the process.

As you learn about and embark on the process, I invite you to read this section as:

- a person who is teaching or leading in uncertain times;
- a learner who is unlearning any limiting beliefs, behaviors, or practices;
- someone who lives in a toxic culture that causes trauma and who may be healing from their own trauma;
- a human being who is invited to bring their full self (emotionally, mentally, spiritually, physically, etc.) to this work;
- an adult with an inner child of their own who needs protection, love, and support.

Exploring these stages while wearing these various hats will allow you to examine where you are affirmed and where you may need to adjust, change, grow, reflect, or seek support. Take notes with your different hats as headings to track your progress.

As you learn more about the stages, think about where you feel drawn, what you have already experienced, and where you feel resistance. The areas where you feel resistance, ironically, are usually the areas where we need to visit more closely.

In the following sections, I'll walk you through each of the seven stages in the process-driven approach to being trauma responsive: know thyself; know thy curriculum, research, and supporting educational frameworks; bear witness; feel; grieve; initiate; and heal and transform.

Why Does Trauma-Responsive Teaching Begin with Knowing Yourself?

Know thyself were the words that marked the entrance of the Temple of Apollo, home of the Oracle of Delphi. This was the two-word axiom the high priestess wanted to leave with the thousands of people, including kings, queens, statesmen, philosophers, and common people alike who traveled hundreds of miles or more to receive her prophetic guidance every year (Ruiz 2017). Her 2,500-year-old instruction to *Know thyself* is a prerequisite for any educator on their trauma-responsive teaching journey. Many of us can fall into the "it's all about the kids" trap, neglecting ourselves and our needs in the process. One of the reasons we need to know ourselves is because we are worthy of it—and teaching is a relationship. Our teaching shows students how we know, love, and relate to ourselves. It allows us to model how someone stands in their own power, worth, and self-love. When things are about the kids, they are necessarily about us, too. The essential question is, *How are we inviting kids to see how we relate to ourselves and treat ourselves?* Instead of beginning with

> *The areas where you feel resistance, ironically, are usually the areas where we need to visit more closely.*

a "children first" mindset, and dismissing our own growth process in this approach, we, as teachers, must discover who we are at the deepest level and examine our limiting beliefs and practices that prevent us from reaching our full potential in our respective roles.

Always remember that each of us exists in this profession with our own wounds and biases. We carry this pain deep in our core, and if we don't bring it to the surface for healing, we will inevitably perpetuate harm onto our students (Gaffney 2019). There was a time when I didn't know if I could teach anymore because I was healing from acute personal, professional, and societal trauma. But a swift shift took place at a "sisters in education" retreat that I attended. During a mentorship session with Dr. Gloria Ladson-Billings, I confided in her that I didn't know if I could go on because I had too much healing to do, and she said, "We are always healing because we are always acquiring wounds." This was a transformative remark coming from the founding researcher on culturally relevant pedagogy. Her seminal book *The Dreamkeepers* (2009) had been my teaching bible and yet, this part—the recognition of the trauma and the deep knowing of the way that Black people had navigated it in this country for over four hundred years while still keeping hope and progress alive—was humbling to say the least. It was one thing to be informed; it was a totally different thing to be responsive to that information. It became clear to me that the way to heal going forward is to make room for the wounds to breathe in the presence and comfort of community. That's where the liberation resides. I knew that no matter how scary freedom was, it was what I craved most. It was what my colleagues and students deserved most. However, our unaddressed personal, institutional, and societal traumas often imprison us.

Each of us exists in this profession with our own wounds and biases.

Many of us have had childhood trauma (Burke Harris 2018), are experiencing current traumas, work in communities that face adversity, and practice teaching in inequitable systems that can perpetuate harm not only on students but also onto us (Gaffney 2019). Given this information, "[W]e cannot presume that adulthood is a final, 'trauma-free' destination" (Ginwright 2018). This is especially true when we consider the unique experience of teaching during a global pandemic. COVID-19 is a virus that not only activates an immune response, but it also activates a trauma response by turning our attention to all our unhealed wounds and how we manage crises. Prior to 2020, "[M]uch of our training and practice [was] directed at young people's healing but rarely focused on the healing that is required of adults to be an effective youth practitioner" (Ginwright 2018). When I left New Orleans to be a global teacher educator in 2016, I was shocked to see how few people outside of New Orleans were actually doing the equitable, personal, and systemic work of being trauma informed. That's when I started to formally develop and share these stages, which have been piloted in sixty schools, twenty districts, and thirty-three different locations, both nationally and internationally. The stages have helped educators to do the inner work alongside students to heal. I have learned that many of us are hurting, and it would be hypocritical to try to help students without helping ourselves as we model how we grow through that process.

There are students who may activate a chronic stress response from an unearthed trauma within us. I remember having this kind of experience with a student of my own. I had attended a professional development session where someone shared a powerful quote from Russel Barkley on a slide during her presentation: "[C]hildren who need the most love ask for it in the most unloving ways." I started to believe this and began asking myself how I could teach a particular child who didn't seem to feel *loved*. Melanie, who was new to the class, would come in each day and ask how she could help. She'd try to stay inside with me during lunch and recess instead of going outside and engaging with her peers. She would bring me presents and notes. If I misplaced my phone, she knew exactly where I left it because she was watching my every move. Her social awareness competency was exceptional. She seemed to have mastered knowing what others would say, feel, or do. I found her attention and affection off-putting because while she was so attentive to my needs, I noticed that she often neglected her own needs and responsibilities. Her assignments weren't complete, she always had a reason why she hadn't finished her work, and when I would try to confer with her about her work, she'd cry upon receiving any adjusting feedback. I didn't know what she had been through or how to support her with this, and so I began to research and plan a teachable moment. Little did I know, I would be learning just as much as Melanie if not more.

After reading Section 1, I imagine you recognize that my student Melanie was showing a fawn trauma response. In an effort to support her through this, I did a vulnerable morning meeting lesson on limiting beliefs. In Figure 3–2 you'll find the lesson. I invite you to activate your inner child and go through the lesson, as someone who is your students' age. Notice what limiting beliefs come up for you. Then, you can reflect alongside me as I watched what happened to my own students.

FIGURE 3–2 *Limiting Beliefs Lesson—Part 1*

PARTS/CONTEXT	MORNING MEETING
Opening	Welcome to our community. Today, in part one of this lesson, we are going to explore limiting beliefs, and then in part two, we will think about the ways we can turn those limiting beliefs into expanding beliefs.
Concept overview	First let's discuss what a limiting belief is: a limiting belief is a story we say inside our minds and our hearts that keeps us feeling small, fearful, not enough, and unsupported.
	For example, you may say, "I am not smart enough" when you don't get the score you wanted on a test. Or you may say, "I am not tall enough" when you think of a sport you want to play, or "I am not pretty enough" when you compare yourself to someone else.
	Limiting beliefs make us feel stuck, or they make us feel worse about the things we are experiencing. Limiting beliefs don't only come from us, they can also come from our family, friends, and even teachers who say hurtful things without even realizing how harmful their words could be. They may say things like, "You're too short" or "You're so mean" or "You're not good at . . ." These comments can feel like a blow to our hearts and minds, whether someone else says them to us or we are saying them to ourselves.

(continues)

(continued)

PARTS/CONTEXT	MORNING MEETING
Practicing the activity	▶ Take a moment to think about a limiting belief you may have. It may have come from your inner voice, from a family member or a friend, or even from a teacher. No matter where it came from, it makes you feel like you're not good enough and it also makes you feel unsupported. ▶ Write that limiting belief down. Then, write about the situation. And finally, write the story. ▶ Start with the least amount of scaffolding and then give the students an example if you need to increase the scaffold with a demonstration. ▶ (You'll see my example after I share Melanie's.)
Melanie's example	**Limiting belief:** "I am not worthy!" **Situation:** "Coming to this school in fourth grade after you've already become a family with all of my classmates since they were in kindergarten." **Story:** "When I came to this school, I was so sad and scared. I moved here from Baton Rouge with my mom to stay with my grandma because my dad went to jail. I was so sad that my family broke up. My heart hurt because my daddy's in trouble. When I came here, you were so close to the class, I never saw a teacher be so lovely. I wanted to be a part of the family, but I didn't feel worthy because I haven't been with you since kindergarten like the other kids and I am not as smart as them."

Melanie's words were a piercing reflection. My heart swelled with compassion for her, her loss, her grief, and her desire to fit in. I set up a healing space, but I didn't know if I was ready to learn what was behind her fawn trauma response. It turns out I had written the same limiting belief in my own journal: "I am not worthy!" The first time I felt that way was when I told my guidance counselor that I wanted to go to Sarah Lawrence College for writing. Instead of encouraging me, he told me I couldn't afford it, I would never be accepted, and I would never get married there. I remember feeling defeated at sixteen years old and wondering what marriage had to do with my educational desires. Earlier that year, I learned he went to Vassar College, a similar liberal arts school. I thought he'd celebrate my ambition and support my quest. Instead, he extinguished my fire and placed doubt in my heart. Years later, I was still asking myself the same question as Melanie when in professional spaces: Am I worthy?

I made a choice to share that reflection with her. "Melanie, I have the same belief!" Instead of telling her about the high school story, I thought of another moment in kindergarten. It was the first day of school. I was so excited because I didn't go to pre-K and I was the last of the three children in my family to go to school. My mother brought me to school that morning and had breakfast with me in the cafeteria. Then she walked me to class, I rushed her out by saying, "I am OK, mom! I am a big girl, you can go!" My mom smiled and said these words before she left: "Be a good girl and listen to your teacher. Remember, a teacher can be like a second mom to you." After hugging my mom, I rushed past the crying children. I was perplexed by their tears! "We're in school. What's there to cry about?" I thought. I gave myself a classroom tour as the teacher pried sobbing children away from their caregivers. My fingers traced the rims of the picture books with great anticipation for the stories. Then, my teacher invited us to sit down as she did attendance. She went through the list once, calling all names and counting all the students. Then she went through the list another time, calling all names and counting the students. "Something's not right," she said. "I know everyone's here," she continued. "Arlene, Arlene, Arlene . . ."

"My name is pronounced AR-LENN, that's what my daddy named me. There's an *accent grave* (è) on the first *e*," I responded with pride.

"Oh, I see. I remember your mom. She had a very heavy accent. You all are not from here. You're in America now. In school, you're AR-LEEN."

I remember feeling not worthy of being who I was born to be. I remember feeling like I had to be someone else in school to be accepted by my teacher. I remember wanting my mom to come back or wanting to start wailing like one of those tearful children.

Maybe they knew intuitively that school was not a safe place before I could learn that from experiencing this first encounter with my first teacher.

Melanie responded to my sharing by saying, "That's horrible, Ms. Casimir. Maybe that's why you're such a powerful teacher. I want you to know that *you* don't make me feel unworthy like your teacher did to you. The time you spent with the kids before me makes me feel unworthy."

This healing encounter was a game changer for Melanie and for me. She was the student I was having the most difficulty with and, ironically, she also had the same wound or limiting belief as I did. Hers was developed under different circumstances but was still the same belief nonetheless. I could have kept my limiting belief to myself but it would have kept our healing on the surface. Having come up with some examples of my own where I experienced institutional trauma in school allowed me to decide which example I could share to heal forward with my students. You can do the same thing. Take time "offstage" to consider limiting beliefs you developed as a school-aged child.

Students shared heart-wrenching things like "I am not capable of learning," "My mother doesn't love me," "I'm ugly," "I am bad," "I am slow." It's so important to treat their words like a broken mosaic only they can put together as a window to see things in their life differently. In part two of the meeting (shown in Figure 3–3), we learned about expanding beliefs.

FIGURE 3–3 *Limiting Beliefs Lesson—Part 2*

PARTS/CONTEXT	MORNING MEETING
Ground in	Let's come back together and feel where those limiting beliefs exist in our bodies. I find that mine lives in my throat. I feel like that feeling got stuck there. Where can you spot the feeling of your limiting belief in your body? Now, let's practice sending the breath to those areas. Breathe in and out until you feel like you've taken a peaceful breathing bath. Try to let go and release that feeling into the air.

PARTS/CONTEXT	MORNING MEETING
Concept overview	Now, let's discuss what an expanding belief is: an expanding belief is a story we say inside our minds and our hearts that helps us to feel like we are accepted, capable, enough, loved, and supported just the way we are.
	We create expanding beliefs by turning our limiting belief into an affirmation that helps us to feel better about ourselves until we believe it. It may sound like:
	▶ I am good enough!
	▶ I am worthy!
	▶ I am beautiful!
	▶ I am the perfect height!
	▶ I am capable of learning!
	Expanding beliefs make us feel good enough. They help us to see that we are the authors of our lives. We can teach our inner voice to speak to us in loving ways even if we learned how to speak to ourselves in unloving ways because of a teacher, family member, friend, or our hurting inner voice.
Practicing the activity	Take your limiting belief and turn it into an expanding belief. It should make you feel like you're enough, like you're encouraged, loved, and supported to be the best you can be.
	Then write a *new* situation. What do you want to happen now that you have this expanding belief? What do you want to be true moving forward? And last, write the story of how you will talk to yourself now.
	(Start with the least amount of scaffolding and then give the students an example, if you need to, increase the scaffold with a demonstration. You'll see my example after I share Melanie's.)

(continues)

(continued)

PARTS/CONTEXT	MORNING MEETING
Melanie's example	**Expanding belief:** "I *am* worthy!" **Situation:** "I am new to this school but I belong here like everyone else." **The story I am choosing to tell myself:** "No matter what is happening with my family at home, I am worthy. No matter if I am new here, I am worthy. Even if school is hard, I am worthy of a good education. I am studying hard so that I can build a school where I show other students that they are worthy, too."

As we explore limiting beliefs with students, emotions may surface that cause students to cry, tear up, and avoid the conversation. Offer them grace, flexibility, and love. This work is tender and tears are cleansing. They represent the pent-up emotions that come with carrying beliefs that keep us small. Have a box of tissues ready and invite students to breathe, pause, and even take a break and return later if it gets too challenging. The best way to do this well is to go through the process off-stage, before you meet with students, and come up with different examples from your own childhood experiences. Ask yourself:

- What is the limiting belief?
- What kind of trauma is this limiting belief tied to from my childhood?
- Where did this limiting belief come from (me, a family member, a friend, a teacher, a stranger, etc.)?
- Where do I feel this limiting belief in my body? (What tenses up?)
- How does it feel to turn this limiting belief into an expanding belief?
- Where do I want to put my expanding belief so that I can see it?
- What is the story I want to tell myself now that I have this expanding belief?

- What are some of the insights and revelations you are having about yourself, your life, and your experiences after engaging in these lessons?

- Completing these questions before working with your students on limiting and expanding beliefs will allow you to engage in this exercise with authenticity, compassion, grace, flexibility, and transparency.

We can teach our inner voice to speak to us in loving ways even if we learned how to speak to ourselves in unloving ways because of a teacher, family member, friend, or our hurting inner voice.

Why Doing This Work Offstage Matters

As explored in Courtney's section, we may also experience secondary traumatic stress from teaching in communities that are facing adversity and/or by witnessing students with trauma of their own. If we do not discover who we are and care for ourselves, we can hurt others unintentionally. So how can we be trauma responsive in our classrooms and schools when we are often experiencing personal trauma, vicarious trauma, and burnout? How can we be there for

For more about secondary traumatic stress, see Section 2, pp 44–46

our own families, our school communities, and our students? It's important that we engage in offstage healing work similarly to how we prepare our academic lessons offstage. As we attempt to build healthy relationships with our students onstage, our own healing and well-being need to be prioritized, practiced, and valued at the same time.

How Does a Culturally Relevant and Trauma-Informed Perspective Impact My Ability to Respond?

Given the brutal facts of New Orleans' failing educational system prior to Hurricane Katrina, and how my students fit into that puzzle, Alfred Adler's inferiority complex concept is quite the fitting diagnosis for the identity crisis that children in marginalized communities endure. The Austrian psychologist wrote that educators must believe in the power of their students and channel their resources to support their students in experiencing their inherent power. I am a strong advocate for this remedy.

To implement a trauma-responsive approach, it is essential to cultivate a trauma-informed perspective and to understand the principles that guide your actions. As Courtney explains in Section 2, trauma-responsive classrooms are good for everyone. By shifting from "What's wrong with this student?" to "What has happened to this student?" (Winfrey and Perry 2021) and ultimately to "What's right with this student?" we go from deficit thinking to asset-based thinking in our perspective. It is important to be prepared to support students who are experiencing or who have experienced trauma, even if we do not know who they are. Nor should we assume that a child is experiencing trauma because of their economic, emotional, or behavioral difficulties. A student does not need to disclose their trauma or the institutional harms affecting them to be supported (Venet 2021). Instead, we can realize the signs and be proactive in our response.

> *By shifting from "What's wrong with this student?" to "What has happened to this student?" (Winfrey and Perry 2021) and ultimately to "What's right with this student?" we go from deficit thinking to asset-based thinking in our perspective.*

Thinking about what's right with all our students and what's right within their communities, and being aware of the collective injustices they face, helps us organize the principles to solidify our mindsets and guide our trauma-responsive approach.

When teaching in New Orleans, the guiding principles of trauma-informed schools from the Substance Abuse and Mental Health Services Administration (SAMHSA 2014) helped me take an inquiry stance. As I ask and answer the following questions, I invite you to think about how this stance can help you to respond to the students in your community. In the list below, the **bold words** are from SAMHSA's 2014 framework on trauma-informed care. I created six questions to bring these principles to life in my classroom. I hope that these questions will help you to bring these principles to life in your own classroom, as well:

1. How can I cocreate a classroom/school community that prioritizes my students' cultural, emotional, mental, physical, and spiritual **safety**?

2. How can I cultivate **trustworthiness and transparency** with my classroom/school procedures, policies, and practices?

3. What are some of the **gender, cultural, and historical issues** that my students are facing? What are some of the other social justice issues they are facing now and how am I cultivating their critical consciousness around these issues in my teaching?

4. How can I cocreate classroom protocols that center **peer support** throughout academic, social, and emotional learning?

5. What would authentic **collaboration and mutuality** with my students, colleagues, caregivers, and community look like, sound like, and feel like? What would we hear, see, feel, and do?

6. How can I center their inherent power, **voice, and choice** in every decision I make?

My work on trauma-responsive pedagogy expands on the SAMHSA principles by weaving in the inner work of educator healing. In addition to the questions above, I thought about the ways I could reflect on how to hold space for myself and my own process off stage. I knew there was no way to give what I hadn't experienced or developed within myself. The following questions are my expansion to the SAMHSA principles and an invitation for you to engage in the inner work:

1. Where do I feel **safe** in my school building and in my practice as an educator and why?

2. Who do I **trust** and feel like I can be **transparent** with about my wins and challenges in my school or greater educational community? How trustworthy and transparent is my administration, and how does the way administrators engage with faculty and staff affect my teaching?

3. What are some of the **gender, cultural, and historical issues** that my colleagues and I are facing?

4. How supported do I feel by my **peers** and what protocols do we have in place to collaborate (for example, intravisitations, cross-grade-level planning, common prep times, professional learning communities)?

5. How do I express my autonomy, professional license, and creativity in my work? When do I feel free to make decisions that are best for me and for my students?

Answering these questions helps us to see where we are trying to give from a healed or a wounded place. If we are trying to dismantle oppression without doing the necessary inner work, we run a high risk of replicating oppression. Oftentimes, we can perpetuate the harm we are experiencing. If we don't feel empowered to exercise our own autonomy, we may create classroom spaces where students do not take ownership of their learning because they know, be it subconsciously or consciously, that they are not invited to make decisions independently.

> *If we are trying to dismantle oppression without doing the necessary inner work, we run a high risk of replicating oppression.*

How Can I Weave Trauma-Responsive Pedagogy into the Fabric of My Instruction?

As educators, many of us need to disrupt the notion that only the teacher and school choose the curriculum and culture—that it is solely in our hands to determine what students would learn and how. I knew that operating in this traditional way, particularly with Black and brown students and families, was a form of colonization and an implementation of white supremacy culture (Okun 2021). By this, I mean going into a community we knew nothing about and telling them what their values should be to achieve what we considered to be success. This is especially true in schools in underserved communities or serving Black, Indigenous, and people of color. I often asked myself: If these children were from white affluent families, would we tell their parents what to value and would we define success for them? Would we tell them to "*work hard and be nice*" instead of addressing the systemic issues that cause them to be frustrated and weary? When implemented, all of the tenets of white supremacy culture are harmful to the communities we profess to support. Instead, we can ask ourselves: How can we move from a system of colonization and domination to a system of care, healing, love, and trust in what the people we serve want for themselves. We can offer an expanded or enlightened view of the world and the opportunities within it. However, our perception of success should never take precedence over caregivers, families, and students.

Stage 1: Know Thyself

Developing self-awareness is inner work. Some nonexhaustive, concrete ways you could get to know yourself and cultivate more self-awareness include:

- going to therapy; (be it talk therapy, spiritual therapy, a support group with therapeutic accents, or somatic therapy)
- journaling;
- engaging in an embodiment practice that invites you to be present in your body like yoga, breath work, dance, or any kind of movement where you are fully present;
- engaging in a spiritual practice like meditation, prayer, a nature walk, taking yourself on an "artist date" (Cameron 1992).

If you want to know yourself better, start with paying attention to your self-talk. How does your inner voice perceive your life experiences? Is your inner critic louder than your inner child (Arrien 1993)? Are you kind to yourself? Do you engage with yourself like a loving friend? What do you notice about how you feel in your body? How much time do you have to spend alone? Do you feel like you can take time for yourself? Is the way you perceive yourself the same way others perceive you? Phone a friend or trusted family member. What do they have to say about you? Craft some specific questions you could ask them, like: *What do you think I value? What is a strength of mine? Where do you think I could develop myself? What kind of advice would you seek from me? What's your fondest memory of me and what did it tell you about my personality or character?*

These reflections could help you get close to your authentic core and be in integrity with who you are as a person and as an educator (Palmer 1998). Next, we'll learn how having a culturally relevant and trauma-responsive perspective can impact our ability to respond to our students. We'll answer questions by taking an inquiry stance to assist us in examining how SAMHSA's trauma-informed principles can play out in our specific classroom and school context.

Stage 2: Know Thy Content (in the Context of Culturally Relevant and Trauma-Responsive Pedagogy)

If we are not solid in our instructional knowledge and skills, it doesn't matter how self-aware or socially aware we are; we will not be able to respond to our students' trauma in an academic, social, and emotional context. To weave trauma-responsive pedagogy into the fabric of your instruction, however, you need also to know your content through a culturally relevant (Ladson-Billings 1995) and trauma-responsive lens. This is about getting to know your content in a new context and deepening your reflection to integrate the principles in a healing-centered (Ginwright 2018) way. Figure 3–4 has some questions you can ask yourself to gauge the knowledge you have around how you could make your content more culturally relevant and trauma responsive.

FIGURE 3–4 *Questions to Help You Know Thy Content*

- What is your instructional content (i.e., subject, standards, and skills)?

- What is the research behind it (pedagogy, methodology, theory, and practices)? Which demographic has the research been studied with?

- What are the educational frameworks that inform your curriculum and school culture (e.g., culturally relevant teaching, equity, social-emotional learning, trauma-informed teaching)? How inclusive are those frameworks and how do you implement them?

(continues)

- How do you see trauma responses manifesting for you and for your students when teaching this content area? Why?

- What kind of institutional oppression/trauma do you need to deconstruct and/or disrupt to give your students full access to themselves in your classroom or school community?

Evaluating your responses to these questions can support you with finding opportunities to integrate the guiding trauma-informed principles and other inclusive educational frameworks into the fabric of your teaching. You can integrate these principles into any curriculum. I suggest you start with a curriculum you are familiar with. For me it is balanced literacy, a form of literacy instruction that blends phonemic awareness, phonics, authentic text reading, and comprehension skills, with an emphasis on student engagement. For example, to design and implement an inclusive trauma-informed balanced literacy curriculum that was grounded in culturally relevant pedagogy, social-emotional and healing-centered learning, as well as social justice, I asked myself:

- What are the components of balanced literacy?
- Where can I weave trauma-responsive practices into an already packed day?

Then I asked myself:

- How do I want to teach balanced literacy?
- Which methods would I use and which pedagogies would inform my methodology?

I thought about the parts, structure, skills, and strategies in the curriculum and about what needed to be deconstructed to meet the vision that was emerging from this groundwork. For example, reading picture books with my students, I came to realize that many culturally relevant texts were not only mirrors where my students could see themselves or windows where they could see others (Bishop 1990); some of these texts were also a healing balm helping students to process difficult experiences and emotions in community.

This led me to create a "healing book talk protocol" and a Stories as Medicine framework for teaching read-aloud lessons.

For more on the Stories as Medicine framework for teaching read-aloud lessons, see the online resources.

In this framework, I use a text set addressing a social issue that could cause trauma around any aspect of my students' identity. I focus on presenting the text with transferable prompts that could be used across the texts. I also made the decision to cultivate my students' critical consciousness (Gay and Kirkland 2003) and to create a shared pool of meaning by considering the conceptual lexicon that would drive our discussions. The three concepts that drove our work across texts were: wounded, healing, and witnessing. *Wounded* was defined as any hurt, be it physical, mental, emotional, financial, spiritual, racial, cultural, and so on. We talked about the wounds we can see and the more subtle wounds of society. *Healing* was defined as the steps we take to get better through "treatment" and time. *Witnessing* was defined as the way we paused to see what characters experienced. In story arcs, there would always be trouble for a character to resolve. And that meant that there would always be things to think about in picture books with great story arcs that could lend themselves to healing or Stories as Medicine:

- Who is wounded in the story?
- How do we know?
- Why are they wounded?
- How do they heal?
- Who is witnessing their healing?
- How can this story help you, a friend, or this community?

As students became more familiar with these concepts, they began to consider the many kinds of wounds characters experience (emotional, mental, physical, relational, and spiritual to name a few). We talked about wounds in poetic ways and carried the metaphor of wounded and healing across many texts and even into our conversations about peer engagement and relationships. During our healing book talks, children began sharing what was wounding them. As a teacher, I also shared how I managed the loss of my grandfather. Students shared the loss of their family members. In the same way, so many children today know loss because of COVID-19. In New Orleans, students knew loss because of natural disasters, gun violence, displacement, housing insecurity, and a rapidly changing educational landscape. It was a space to process and heal.

Of course, there were times where I had to honor my role as a mandated reporter, bring in administration, and reach out to the school social worker or a school psychologist. There were times when we had to call families in. This is to be expected. Healing work is collective and communal. It's important to share this with families and invite them along with supportive organizations to do this work alongside us because it truly takes a village to transform. As you heal and invite children to do the same, many wounds can surface for healing. Instead of shying away, leverage the community for support to assist children in what they share.

Even beautiful stories can bring up wounds for children if they feel the absence of the beauty of the story in their own lives.

I remember reading the story "Homemade Love" by bell hooks (2002) to a group of second graders, when a child said, "My mother doesn't love me like the little girl's mother loves her in this book." At that moment, her teacher blushed and said, "Don't say that; that's not true." Sometimes students will share things that make us uncomfortable to imagine that they feel that way. Instead of silencing and dismissing them, it's important to honor what they share and ask questions like:

- What makes you feel that way?
- Is that a limiting belief or an expanding belief or both? (Refer to the lesson earlier in the section on this.)
- What would make you feel like . . . ?
- How can I support you?
- How do you feel after sharing what's on your heart and mind?

Even beautiful stories can bring up wounds for children if they feel the absence of the beauty of the story in their own lives. Beautiful stories can be a painful reminder of what was or what will never be. Engaging in trauma-responsive healing work is all about how we frame and facilitate the read-aloud and the healing book talk.

Stage 3: Bear Witness: Entering Our Classroom and Schools with a Trauma-Responsive Lens

When people ask me how I see the pandemic impacting our educational system, I often respond by saying, "This is a global crisis and we will be processing different stages of trauma for decades to come." While this may seem grim to some, I see it as an invitation to heal. An invitation to heal individually, collectively, and globally from all the injustices that have haunted us for centuries. But I didn't always know that, sometimes, healing hurts more than the injury. As I mentioned earlier, ancient wisdom traditions call this process a "healing crisis." Trauma-responsive teachers need a professional and personal container to hold space for this process. We need support with inner and outer work because *every healing journey begins with a healing crisis.* Let me tell you about mine.

Trauma is not new to me. You see, I was born into a family who experienced a great deal of trauma for generations. From the unstable conditions and institutions that govern my parents' native land, Haiti, to immense poverty and lack of access to essential resources, to natural disasters that brought famine and despair. My father told me stories of Hurricane Flora, seeing crops dry up on his parents' farm, cattle falling like flies, and eating mangoes for breakfast, for lunch, and with salt for dinner because they were strong enough to grow in the dry soil. He told me stories of the Haitian revolution and how his country is still paying for their freedom and still is made an example of today for wanting autonomy. He told these stories during the crack epidemic when we saw people jumping out of windows, bodies twisting under the influence, and unstable times. He told these stories between shifts, working two to three jobs and still making time to read, laugh, dance, and sing. Through my lived experience and research, I have learned that trauma takes many forms, and whether inherited or newly acquired, shapes who we are and how we react to the environment around us. Yet our story doesn't have to be set in stone. We can always tap into an inner well, consider the facts, and rewrite the story into a narrative of post-traumatic growth and victory in the face of challenges. This is what my father taught me.

I tell this story to frame this subsection of bearing witness. To me, bearing witness is the ability to look, listen, and learn from another person's experience with compassion, not empathy. I see empathy as the projection of an emotion onto an object, whereas compassion is an invitation to look at someone's humanity and to listen to their story with attention, care, and love. Thank you for listening to and seeing me. I grew up in Brooklyn, New York, with two Haitian immigrant parents who came to America to obtain the American dream. We soon learned that the trauma would not subside, and therefore we had to tap into inner resources to heal. That's why the reminder from Dr. Gloria Ladson-Billings that "we are always healing because we are always acquiring wounds" was so striking. It brought me back to some of my own wounds and helped me to remember how I transmuted them. One of the things my parents sought to provide is stability, the comfort of a home, and a transformative education that could support us in transcending our circumstances. So, that's why my parents were shocked when I decided to go to New Orleans to teach the first children to come to school after Hurricane Katrina. Yes, they were proud; yes, they were supportive; but they were also worried that I'd be walking into what they tried desperately to leave behind. And this is where my healing journey began.

> *Compassion is an invitation to look at someone's humanity and to listen to their story with attention, care, and love.*

What do I know now because of my education, experience, research, and wisdom? I know a lot about trauma and how it takes root to rob a community of its ability to cope and thrive. When people ask me to explain how I see trauma manifesting and being solidified in schools and organizations, I often share three ways the negative effects of prolonged stress responses turn into sustained trauma responses and sometimes even irreconcilable crises that negatively impact the community:

- Trauma is solidified when your community fails to witness your suffering. The implicit expectation is for you to deal with your pain privately or be punished for not moving on with business as usual.

- Trauma is solidified when trauma-exposure responses and how they manifest for adults and children alike in classrooms and schools are dismissed, ignored, or ridiculed.

- Trauma is when something happens in your life that is against your will and you're left to deal with the stress and residue of the experience without the proper community support to cope effectively.

Clearly, trauma is not a full stop, although in many instances it is treated as such. Trauma is something we respond to, and the first way to respond is to notice the call. Figure 3–5 shows the many types of trauma that we may be experiencing alongside our students.

FIGURE 3–5 *Types of Trauma*

TYPE(S) OF TRAUMA	MANIFESTATION	NONEXHAUSTIVE EXAMPLE(S)
Generational	Traumatic experiences and maladaptive trauma responses that are passed down in families for generations (Davidson and Mellor 2001)	▶ Alcoholism in a family ▶ Domestic violence
Individual	Adverse personal experiences that take place in someone's childhood or adulthood that affect their ability to cope (Felitti et al. 1998)	▶ Abuse ▶ Neglect
Familial	Traumatic experiences that take place and destabilize an entire family's ability to cope and heal	▶ Death of a loved one ▶ Incarceration ▶ Presence of mental illness ▶ Homelessness ▶ Deportation

TYPE(S) OF TRAUMA	MANIFESTATION	NONEXHAUSTIVE EXAMPLE(S)
Communal	Traumatic experiences that affect a particular neighborhood or city's ability to cope and heal	▶ When someone is harmed in a community ▶ Gentrification ▶ Our nation's response to Hurricane Katrina, the water issue in Flint, Michigan, etc.
Relational	Traumatic experiences that are activated in our relationships (Isobel et al. 2019)	▶ Between a student and teacher ▶ Between partners ▶ Between siblings ▶ Between friends ▶ Between colleagues
Societal	Traumatic experiences that affect the entire nation	▶ The stress epidemic in our nation ▶ The mental health crisis in our nation ▶ The substance abuse issues in our nation
Collective	Traumatic circumstances and experiences that affect the entire world's ability to cope or, as Hirschberger (2018) writes, "[S]hatters the basic fabric of society" (1)	▶ War ▶ Terrorism ▶ Mass shootings ▶ Global pandemics ▶ World hunger

(continues)

(continued)

TYPE(S) OF TRAUMA	MANIFESTATION	NONEXHAUSTIVE EXAMPLE(S)
Cultural	Traumatic experiences produced by countries and people in positions of power who harm and oppress people from a different culture with their words, actions, laws, and policies, often in "conflicts with other cultures or divergent subgroups of the same culture" (Stamm et al. 2004, 1)	► When the 45th president said that coronavirus was the Chinese virus, we witnessed the harm this caused Asians; this perception activated the hatred in people's hearts to retaliate
Historical and racial	Traumatic experiences that disproportionately affect a specific group of people because of their race (Saleem et al. 2020)	► Police brutality ► Redlining ► Discrimination
Economic	Traumatic experiences due to a lack of resources	► Lack of access to people, places, and things that would improve someone's quality of life ► World hunger ► World poverty
Institutional	Traumatic experiences that take place in spaces where you are meant to learn and grow	► Being punished when you are in pain ► Not being exposed to your own history and culture in your curriculum ► Active shooter drills
	Traumatic experiences that take place in spaces that are designed to serve the public and instead harm and oppress the people who are in those public spaces	► The criminal "injustice" system ► The lack of access to health care for all Americans ► COVID-19 ► Global warming

Which of these types of trauma have manifested in your life and in the lives of the students who you support? Take stock and notice how akin trauma is to matryoshka dolls from Russia. When there's a trauma, we can usually open it up and notice another trauma beneath it. The personal traumas that we experience are often nestled in larger collective and societal trauma. They are not ours to excavate alone or to process once a week with a therapist. These are circumstances that we face on a daily basis that need to be addressed in our learning communities so that we may heal and transform them.

Witness (Don't Guide, Don't Teach, Be Present, and Watch)

What happens when we don't bear witness? When we don't bear witness, we disassociate and our body, mind, and spirits become disconnected. We find ourselves unaware of what we are experiencing or feeling. When we don't bear witness, we neglect our humanity, our students' humanity, and that of the world. When we don't bear witness, the negative effects of trauma are solidified. When we don't bear witness, crisis consumes us. When we don't bear witness, we get swept into the next catch-all phrases and movements in education. Soon we will see trauma-informed, trauma-sensitive, trauma-focused educational movements, but the question is what do we see right in front of us, right on our screens, right in our lives? What has heart and meaning for us (Lantieri 2002), and how is this new reality shaping our pedagogy? We need to bring a discerning eye to our work. We are often told what the latest (medical, psychological, clinical, educational, and interpersonal) research is, and without a thought we begin implementing these approaches only on the surface out of mandates. Social-emotional learning, trauma-informed teaching, culturally relevant pedagogy, universal design learning; What do they mean for you and your practice? Dr. Aurelie Athan, a professor in my clinical psychology and education program, often asks, "What is research, but 'me' search?" How are we witnessing our own lives? When we bear witness, we can pay attention to what's happening inside of us, around us, and within our students. That's what the critically acclaimed researchers and theorists have done.

What are the ways to bear witness? Don't guide, don't teach, be present, and watch. As Dr. Elizabeth Dutro writes, classrooms can be sites of testimony and witness to trauma (2019). Dutro further explains what it means to "witness others' lives" (6). It's far from straightforward. To witness we must be present. Nothing matters but the current moment when you are present. Not the past. Not the future. You're not working in multiple browsers, and if your child, partner or spouse, or anyone else crosses the screen, you're present with that too. To witness we must listen. If you were to rearrange the letters of the word *listen*, the same letters can form the word *silent*. When we are silent, we can witness our own testimonies and that of our students. It could be in a comment in a turn-and-talk, a journal entry, or even a writing assignment—the way they respond to a call. When we listen and we are able to silence our mind, we can hear what's emerging for our students. We can address trauma in everyday teaching and learning.

During these times we are witnessing, we must bring an open heart, vulnerability, and fierce analysis and advocacy to this work with children. We must bear witness to our lives. And we must also witness what's happening in the world. Pause to reflect and to think:

- What are you witnessing outside of your window?
- On the news?
- In your social media feeds?
- In your neighborhood?
- In your home?
- In your classroom?

MOMENT OF REFLECTION

What are the images, metaphors, and words that come to mind for you when you think about witnessing the trauma that you are experiencing and how witnessing relates to your role in addressing trauma in your classroom, school, and beyond?

One of the ways that I invite students and school communities to bear witness to one another is by using the holding space protocol shown in Figure 3–6. This protocol has been used in grades K–8, in professional

A printable version of Holding Space Protocol is available in the online resources.

development meetings, in family engagement meetings, and in leadership teams. It's an opportunity to set the tone of the day or meeting by letting children and adults know "I see you," "I want to support you as long as I have the capacity to do so," and "I am listening." This is a protocol that's implemented best when it is introduced with the facilitator or teacher being willing to allow students to witness them. For example, I often think of the most authentic and vulnerable thing I could share with students while still maintaining my composure, privacy, and poise. That means

FIGURE 3–6 *Holding Space Protocol*

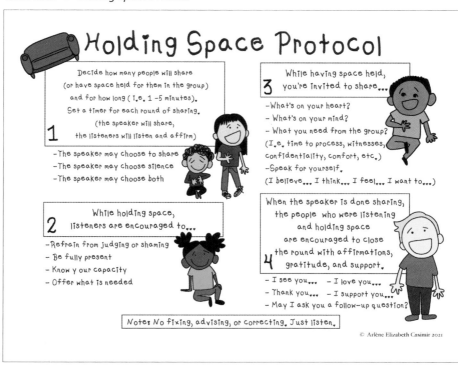

that I will not share something that feels too overwhelming to discuss. I give myself time to come up with ideas of what to share with colleagues and with students.

Also, this practice works best in morning meetings, closing meetings, or after recess. If teaching in clusters, however, it helps to implement this protocol during the first few minutes of class. Many colleagues have adapted this by creating a schedule where two or three children share a day. I noticed that many schools have two assigned children and one open spot as a walk-in invitation for a student who needs space held that day. It's important to note that consistency becomes the fertile soil for more introverted students to grow and share once they see something like this implemented daily.

Stage 4: Feel: Tending to the Wounds Within Ourselves and Within Our Classrooms

At this stage, we allow ourselves to feel the depression, anxiety, despair, anger, paranoia, rage, fear, distrust, isolation we are all being called to feel.

There's this saying: "You can't heal it unless you feel it." Now is not the time to dissociate. We are often lured into the traps of productivity, quantity over quality, and workaholism as a way to numb the pain and blind ourselves to the emotions that are surfacing within us. Dissociation tears us apart from healthy human relationships, tears us from connection to our emotions, our body. The more you acknowledge your feelings and do self-care to emotionally regulate and cultivate healthy coping mechanisms, the more able you are to heal.

A healing crisis calls for compassion; sitting in the darkness with the other, feeling the suffering in yourself (as well as in them) and creating a learning space that can alleviate that suffering.

In, *It Didn't Start with You: How Inherited Family Trauma Shapes Who We Are and How to End the Cycle*, Mark Wolynn says, "[A]n essential part of healing involves our ability to incorporate the experiences of our physical sensations into the process. Insight is often gained when we are willing to tolerate what's uncomfortable in the quest to understand ourselves" (2016, 152).

Try It . . .

Think about a recent time when you experienced an uncomfortable or undesirable emotion. Instead of judging the feeling as "bad" and trying to reject or suppress it, embrace the emotion by asking yourself: What happened? What was I doing, thinking, saying, and feeling? Who else was involved? Where does this emotion now live in my body? Once you identify where the emotion is in your body, close or lower your eyes and send several deep breaths to that area. You could feel a sense of release expressed through a sigh, tears, an involuntary movement, or a combination of all reactions. Now, breathe in and out, sending that emotion's energy to your hands. Breathe in and squeeze your hands as if balling up your fists. Breathe out and open your hands to release that emotion. Do this for three to nine breaths until you feel a sense of relief. How does that area in your body feel now? Congratulations, you just took yourself through an exercise in self-compassion by reflecting and breathing through an emotion to transmute it.

We can support our students on their journey by doing this work ourselves. That's when our teaching becomes healing-centered. It starts with us being willing to do the work off-stage. Many of our students are experiencing various crises. Supporting them through any crisis is not done through empathy or witnessing the suffering of another and imagining what this may feel like. A healing crisis calls for compassion, sitting in the darkness with the other, feeling the suffering in yourself (as well as in them), and creating a learning space that can alleviate that suffering.

Compassion is action. It is the belief that someone else's gloom can't put out your own light because you've lit a candle where your pain is—to make meaning of it and to integrate it. Compassion is the awareness that your inner flame can become a lighthouse that helps others return home and whole to themselves. By holding space, listening, and using your light to affirm your students in community, you can facilitate transformation in your classroom.

Stage 5: Grieve . . . It's an Ongoing Process

There are so many emotions that come with loss, and every day we are invited to experience the fullness of our humanity by grappling with those various feelings. Consider a loss you've experienced in your life. What feelings do you recall? Did any of them surprise you? How are you navigating that loss?

As of the writing of this book, I experienced a series of personal tragedies that resulted in me experiencing grief deeply. That made this subsection the most challenging to compose. In full transparency, over the course of twenty-two months, I experienced a divorce, a significant career change, the unexpected loss of my beloved mother, other challenges pertaining to my family, and everything else that was happening in the world during a global pandemic. It became clear that I would really have to embody and integrate the lessons from this chapter in my life to teach and to write about grief from an authentic place. When feeling grief, it can be difficult to see outside of it or even imagine that if you attempt to engage in actions outside of grieving, you are not somehow betraying yourself and those you are grieving. I know this professionally, but these recent events brought this professional knowledge into my personal life. The lessons were incredibly challenging but I was reminded that I could see this as an invitation from beyond to support colleagues, students, and teachers with their own grief. In effort to support students and colleagues with grief, I took note from *Learning from Loss: A Trauma Informed Approach to Supporting Grieving Students* by Brittany R. Collins (2022) for how to talk about loss in the classroom. It became important to define grief, grieving, and healing collectively in each group that I taught, be it educators or children. I started by inviting everyone to share their definitions of the terms to activate their background knowledge and to create a shared pool of meaning.

> *When feeling grief, it can be difficult to see outside of it or even imagine that if you attempt to engage in actions outside of grieving, you are not somehow betraying yourself and those you are grieving.*

Once adults shared their responses, I invited them to engage in a reflection by doing their own grieving inner work before working with students. This could be seen as prework before writing and teaching a lesson:

- How are you holding space for your own grieving?
- How are you holding space for your students' grieving?
- What are you learning about teaching grief and loss in a school setting?
- What were some of your biggest apprehensions, assumptions, and questions about supporting students with loss?

After educators engaged in this reflection, I framed how I teach grieving to students using definitions and the literacy competent of read-alouds. I start with the definitions:

- *grief*—the feelings that come with the loss of a person, place, thing, or experience;
- *grieving*—how you learn to live with that loss (the things you do);
- *healing*—accepting and getting better after a loss (in the context of grieving).

Then I share the read-aloud with characters who are grieving some sort of loss and frame the purpose for reading the text by inviting students to consider:

- Who is grieving in the text?
- How are they grieving (what are some of the things they do, say, or think)?
- Why is grieving important?

Once we are done reading the text and answering questions along the way that are aligned to the text, I invite students to have a grieving talk and apply this concept to their own lives:

- What are you grieving?
- How are you grieving?
- What happens when we don't grieve?

Our society lacks the implementation of grieving rituals in schools. Grieving is such a trauma-responsive practice because it helps people to not be reduced by what has happened to them and instead to process it in community and to move on in ways that honor them.

What has happened is nothing less than healing and transformative. Children have used the space to share the loss of pets, family members, homes, toys, and more. And in doing so, they felt a relief by being able to support each other through the process. I would argue that our society lacks the implementation of grieving rituals in schools. Grieving is such a trauma-responsive practice because it helps people to not be reduced by what has happened to them and instead to process it in community and to move on in ways that honor them. As Collins shares, teachers may not know who is actively grieving in their classrooms. Still we can create a classroom culture that "promotes the well-being of all learners, regardless of whether they have a history of loss or trauma" (Collins 2021, 9).

Stage 6: Initiate the Archetypes

Archetypes are ancient images and symbols that have guided civilization from the beginning of time. From places (like the forest, the castle, the home), to things (like heart, animals, amulets), to selves (like the warrior, queen, father, child), these images have been crucial in understanding the human condition, the individual and collective consciousness.

In a collection of essays entitled *Schools with Spirit*, Linda Lantieri partners with Angeles Arrien to examine the archetypes that teachers embody in schools with spirit. She examines how they have a sense of interconnectedness to themselves, their students, their community, and the world. The four archetypes she delineates are the warrior/leader, the healer, the visionary, and the teacher (2001).

The warrior/leader knows how to show up and marshal their collective resources to get the job done. They are courageous, leading the pack to what feels like a promised land, and even though they may feel fear, they have learned how to create a way where there seems to be no way. The healer is someone who pays attention. They listen to their feelings, they are in touch with their bodies, and they are learning how to transmute their pain, turning wounds into wisdom. The visionary tells the truth. They are able to name the brutal facts, recognize the current reality, and still imagine a future that speaks to the resiliency of humanity. They can see where we need to go and the purpose everyone has in realizing that vision. They know that our world is in a challenging place because many haven't lived their purpose. They invite everyone to be a part of a new world. The teacher sets the stage, and they are open to outcome; they know that the most profound teachable moments happen when you create the right conditions for students to learn and grow. We are always moving through the different archetypes.

Take a moment to journal and reflect on the archetypes:

- When are you the warrior/leader? What kinds of qualities do you embody?

- What kinds of qualities does the healer embody? How can you do that now?

- What kind of vision do you hold for your recovery? For your students? Their families?

- How can your teaching practices support you in holding healing spaces for your colleagues, students, and their families?

It can also be helpful to note how you notice the archetypes manifesting in the people around you. What gifts are they bringing to the table at different times and how can this help you to be more trauma-responsive alongside them?

Stage 7: Heal and Transform: The Intention and Practice of Teaching the Whole Child While Nurturing Your Well-being

In this final stage, we take all that we have learned from trauma-informed care and trauma-responsive pedagogy in the previous sections to experience a healing-centered paradigm shift that promotes transformation in our teaching practices. The purpose of a healing-centered paradigm shift is to recognize that healing is a return to one's authentic self and that school can be the perfect place for restorative and transformative practices (Winn 2020) that help children and faculty to regain wholeness. Some of the guiding principles of healing-centered engagement are holding space, leveraging various healing modalities, and tending to our wounds in effort to heal and transform. By integrating inclusive frameworks such as culturally relevant pedagogy (Ladson-Billings 1995), social-emotional learning, and trauma-responsive pedagogy, we tend to the needs of our students in effort to help them grow holistically. First, we can examine what we know about healing in our own lives.

I know a lot about healing. Healing is helping people get to a state of renewal, wholeness, and well-being (Haga 2020). And it's a process—a nonlinear process that demands us to tap into the depths of our inner being to emerge and reemerge over and over again. Prior to the global pandemic, many of us had never experienced or witnessed a crisis of that magnitude. Even though it has waned in severity and we have already begun to reflect on what we have learned and how to move forward, there is still so much to process. That means that our potential for healing after the pandemic as we continue to cocreate a new normal is far greater than we could have ever wished for.

To heal is not to return to "normal." Many of our schools have been failing for quite some time. They've been ill with injustices that perpetuate trauma for teachers and students alike. We don't have to remain tethered to our previous reality. As Sonya Renee Taylor posted on Instagram, "[W]e will not go back to normal. Normal never was. Our pre-COVID-19 existence was not *normal*; rather, that we *normalized* greed, inequity, exhaustion, depletion, extraction, disconnection, confusion, hoarding, rage, hate, and lack. We should not long to return to normal. We are being given the opportunity to stitch a new garment, one that fits all of humanity and nature" (2020). This applies to the way we run schools, teach our students content, and educate them about life.

> *School can be the perfect place for restorative and transformative practices (Winn 2020) that help children and faculty to regain wholeness.*

We all witnessed some children do better with remote learning when we were all forced to teach from home at the beginning of the pandemic and some children did worse—it all depended on their circumstances.

In *Writing as a Way of Healing*, Louise DeSalvo (1999) teaches how telling our stories can transform our lives. First, we must create a space for wisdom and discernment. Some of the things that we want to cultivate for ourselves is a grounding practice of our own, a community to reflect with, and exercises we can share that can become a salve for our wounds. By doing so even five minutes at a time, we can invite our students to do the same.

I remember teaching a writing class and feeling frustrated by a student who constantly crawled under the table during independent writing time. I couldn't understand why he would do this, and I didn't know how to coach him out of this habit. I wanted to meet with his mother to share my concerns but first I wanted to take a closer look at his writing to learn more about his process before engaging in an intervention. Upon looking at his writing during a one-on-one conference, I noticed that he was writing about seeing his uncle murdered. My heart sank. I brought this up to a colleague and mentor Cornelius Minor who wrote the text *We Got This: Equity, Access and the Quest to Be Who Our Students Need Us to Be* (2019). After reflection, Cornelius said to me: "Some of our students are writing in ink and some of our students are writing in blood. The question is: How do we hold space for our students who are writing in blood?" Once he asked this question, I reflected on the words from his book: "Our job is not to teach our students or even to teach curriculum, our job is to bend the curriculum to meet the needs of our students" (Minor 2019, 101). This led me to grapple with how I would hold space for this student to heal and transform as he wrote about such a traumatic loss. He didn't want to talk about his writing or share it with others. However, his circumstances led me to incorporate a healing share during writing that he could engage in a transformative way. Figure 3–7 gives options for engaging students in a healing share.

FIGURE 3–7 *How to Lead a Healing Share*

OPTIONS FOR A HEALING SHARE	
Let students decide what they are comfortable sharing.	
If students choose to focus on process:	If students choose to focus on product:
▶ What was it like for you to write this piece?	▶ Share your topic.
	▶ Share a line.
▶ What does writing this do for you mentally, emotionally, academically?	▶ Share an excerpt.
▶ Who are you writing this piece for and what do you want them to get from it?	▶ Share your entire piece.
	▶ Share your next steps for revising or editing this piece.
▶ What kinds of lessons are you learning as a result of writing this piece?	

By giving students the option to choose whether or not they would like for their classmates to learn about their process or their product, we de-center the need to be focused solely on the outcome and production of the piece and embrace the journey of writing healing content that can be a salve for students' wounds. Doing so allowed this student to connect with his peers in powerful ways and to work on his piece in a manner that served his growth academically and emotionally.

I have also learned how important it is to let kids be kids. However, often our own inner child has not had the chance to engage in creative ways to heal, and the impact is that we cannot create these conditions for students. In the *Four-Fold Way*, Angeles Arrien (1993) shares how ancient wisdom traditions tend to the traumas of their communities using four universal healing salves:

- storytelling,
- singing,
- silence,
- dancing.

Which of these healing salves are alive in your life and in your class, and which are lying dormant? Which would you like to activate throughout the day? When is the most productive time to do so? Asking ourselves these questions and using these simple tools can help us to cocreate a classroom environment where we are trauma responsive in the service of healing and transformation.

As you come to the closing of this book, may the words in this text be a guiding light in your practice. I hope you can use the knowledge, strategies, and tools you learned to implement trauma-responsive pedagogy with compassion, grace, and flexibility for yourself and your students. Remember, it's a parallel process, and as we say in Haiti, "behind mountains, there are more mountains." So don't strive to arrive. Instead, commit to being present. Enjoy the landscape and savor the lessons learned along the journey.

AFTERWORD

M. Colleen Cruz

*T*he word *trauma* was one of the big buzzwords in the 2019 educational world. It was hard to enter any school or district office without hearing people talking about it. "How do we help *those* kids with trauma?" And although it was a worthy goal to focus on trauma at the school level, there was a way in which trauma was very much a part of the othering of specific children, a way to further separate the practitioners from the pupils.

And then March 2020 arrived and everything changed. In one fell swoop trauma shifted from being about *them* to being about *us*.

In the book you just read, Arlène Elizabeth Casimir and Courtney Baker move the conversation beyond the buzzwords and the othering and into the research and practices school communities can and need to engage in. They let us know that, yes, trauma matters and there are things educators can do to respond to it. And also, perhaps most importantly to me, they firmly, and without hesitation, remind us that all of us are touched by trauma. This was true prepandemic but it has become absolutely impossible to deny now. For us to care for the students we serve, for us to successfully teach them, we must, of course, understand others' trauma and how to respond to it, but also how our own trauma or experiences with others' trauma can have a direct impact on how we respond, teach, and even interact with colleagues and families.

If you're anything like me, the first time I read this book in its entirety, I felt the full weight of everything Arlène and Courtney discussed. There is just so much hurt in our communities, both generationally and in the present moment, it is easy to feel like there's too much for one person to make a difference. But, as I let their words settle, I also realized something very empowering: they have given us the recipe for what to do next period, next week, next school year. Whether it's researched tools for identifying adverse childhood experiences or a protocol for teaching children how to hold space for each other, we are all leaving this book with a large trunk of information, strategies, and ways to take care of our own hearts. I, for one, am incredibly grateful to both Arlène and Courtney for the gift of this book, right at the perfect time. I am thrilled that it is now in the hands of so many educators. I know that the next time I sit in front of a gathered group of children in the classroom, the students and I will be all the better because of this book.

REFERENCES

Achenbach, T. M. 2015. "Developmental Psychopathology." In Blaney, P. H., Krueger, R. F., and Millon, T., eds. *Oxford Textbook of Psychopathology* 3rd edition, 488–512. New York: Oxford University Press.

Adler, A. 2015. *The Education of Children*. Routledge.

Alim, T. N., E. Graves, T. A. Mellman, N. Aigbogun, E. Gray, W. Lawson, and D. S. Charney. 2006. "Trauma Exposure, Posttraumatic Stress Disorder and Depression in an African-American Primary Care Population." *Journal of the National Medical Association* 98(10): 1630–36.

Arrien, A. 1993. *The Four-Fold Way: Walking the Paths of the Warrior, Teacher, Healer, and Visionary*. San Francisco: Harper.

———. 2001. "The Way of the Techer: Principles of Deep Engagement," in *Schools with Spirit: Nurturing the Lives of Children and Teachers,* edited by Linda Lantieri, 148–57. Boston: Beacon Press.

Atlanta Speech School. 2016. "The Atlanta Speech School 'Every Opportunity.'" https://vimeo.com/179818336.

Baker, C. N., S. M. Brown, P. D. Wilcox, J. M. Verlenden, C. L. Black, and B. E. Grant. 2018. "The Implementation and Effect of Trauma-Informed Care Within Residential Youth Services in Rural Canada: A Mixed Methods Evaluation." *Psychological Trauma: Theory, Research, Practice, and Policy* 10: 666–74.

Baker, C. N., H. Peele, M. Daniels, M. Saybe, K. Whalen, S. Overstreet, and The New Orleans Trauma-Informed Schools Learning Collaborative. 2021. "The Experience of COVID-19 and Its Impact on Teachers' Mental Health, Coping, and Teaching." *School Psychology Review* 50 (4): 491–504.

Baker, C. N., M. H. Tichovolsky, J. B. Kupersmidt, M. E. Voegler-Lee, and D. H. Arnold. 2015. "Teacher (Mis) Perceptions of Preschoolers' Academic Skills: Predictors and Associations with Longitudinal Outcomes." *Journal of Educational Psychology* 107(3): 805.

Basile, V., A. York, and R. Black. 2019. "Who Is the One Being Disrespectful? Understanding and Deconstructing the Criminalization of Elementary School Boys of Color." *Urban Education* 0042085919842627.

Bishop, R. S. 1990. "Mirrors, Windows, and Sliding Glass Doors." *Perspectives: Choosing and Using Books for the Classroom* 6 (3).

Beck, A. T. 2002. "Cognitive Models of Depression." *Clinical Advances in Cognitive Psychotherapy: Theory and Application 14* (1): 29–61.

Begeny, J. C., and B. K. Martens. 2006. "Assessing Pre-Service Teachers' Training in Empirically-Validated Behavioral Instruction Practices." *School Psychology Quarterly* 21 (3): 262.

Blodgett, C., and J. D. Lanigan. 2018. "The Association Between Adverse Childhood Experience (ACE) and School Success in Elementary School Children." *School Psychology Quarterly* 33 (1): 137.

Bondy, E., and D. D. Ross. 2008. "The Teacher as Warm Demander." *Educational Leadership* 66 (1): 54–58.

Booth, D., and M. Hachiya, eds. 2004. *The Arts Go to School: Classroom-Based Activities That Focus on Music, Painting, Drama, Movement, Media, and More.* Markham, Ontario, Canada: Pembroke Publishers.

Bowlby, J. 1979. "The Bowlby-Ainsworth Attachment Theory." *Behavioral and Brain Sciences* 2 (4): 637–38.

Briesch, A. M., S. M. Chafouleas, K. Nissen, and S. Long. 2020. "A Review of State-Level Procedural Guidance for Implementing Multi Tiered Systems of Support for Behavior (MTSS-B)." *Journal of Positive Behavior Interventions* 22 (3): 131–44.

Bronfenbrenner, U. 1992. "Ecological Systems Theory." In R. Vasta (Ed.) *Six Theories of Child Development: Revised Formulations and Current Issues*, 187–249. Philadelphia, PA: Jessica Kingsley Publishers.

Brown, S. M., C. N. Baker, and P. Wilcox. 2012. "Risking Connection Trauma Training: A Pathway Toward Trauma-Informed Care in Child Congregate Care Settings." *Psychological Trauma: Theory, Research, Practice, and Policy* 4 (5): 5B l07–515. doi: 10.1037/a0025269.

Burke, N., J. Hellman, B. Scott, C. Weems, and G. Carrion. 2011. "The Impact of Adverse Childhood Experiences on an Urban Pediatric Population." *Child Abuse & Neglect: The International Journal* 35 (6): 408–13.

Cameron, J. 1992. *The Artist's Way: A Spiritual Path to Higher Creativity.* New York: TarcherPerigee.

Caringi, J. C., C. Stanick, A. Trautman, L. Crosby, M. Devlin, and S. Adams. 2015. "Secondary Traumatic Stress in Public School Teachers: Contributing and Mitigating Factors." *Advances in School Mental Health Promotion* 8 (4): 244–56.

Carlson, M., B. Pierce, and W. Thurston. 2020. *Responsive Schools: Building a Trauma Responsive Learning Community for All Children.* Clinical Scholars. https://clinicalscholarsnli .org/projects/responsive-schools-building-a-tauma-responsive -learning-community-for-all-children.

Cassetta, G., and B. Sawyer. 2013. *No More Taking Away Recess and Other Problematic Discipline Practices.* Portsmouth, NH: Heinemann.

Centers for Disease Control and Prevention. 2010. "Adverse Childhood Experiences Reported by Adults—Five States, 2009." *Morbidity and Mortality Weekly Report* 59 (49): 1609.

Centers for Disease Control and Prevention. "The ACE Pyramid." cdc.gov.

Center for Substance Abuse Treatment. 2014. "Understanding the Impact of Trauma." In *Trauma-Informed Care in Behavioral Health Services.* Substance Abuse and Mental Health Services Administration (U.S.).

Chafouleas, S. M., A. H. Johnson, S. Overstreet, and N. M. Santos. 2016. "Toward a Blueprint for Trauma-Informed Service Delivery in Schools." *School Mental Health* 8 (1): 144–62.

Cicchetti, D. 1984. "The Emergence of Developmental Psychopathology." *Child Development* 55(1): 1–7.

Cole, S. F., A. Eisner, M. Gregory, and J. Ristuccia. 2013. *Helping Traumatized Children Learn, Vol. 2: Creating and Advocating for Trauma-Sensitive Schools*. Boston: Massachusetts Advocates for Children.

Collaborative for Academic, Social, and Emotional Learning. n.d. "Advancing Social and Emotional Learning." https://casel.org/.

Collins, B. R. 2022. *Learning from Loss: A Trauma Informed Approach to Supporting Grieving Students*. Portsmouth, NH: Heinemann.

Cornelius-White, J. 2007. "Learner-Centered Teacher-Student Relationships Are Effective: A Meta-Analysis." *Review of Educational Research* 77 (1): 113–43.

Crenshaw, K. W. 2017. *On Intersectionality: Essential Writings*. New York: The New Press.

Cronholm, P. F., C. M. Forke, R. Wade, M. H. Bair-Merritt, M. Davis, M. Harkins-Schwarz, and J. A. Fein. 2015. "Adverse Childhood Experiences: Expanding the Concept of Adversity." *American Journal of Preventive Medicine* 49 (3): 354–61.

Davidson, A. C., and D. J. Mellor. 2001. "The Adjustment of Children of Australian Vietnam Veterans: Is There Evidence for the Transgenerational Transmission of the Effects of War-Related Trauma?" *Australian & New Zealand Journal of Psychiatry* 35 (3): 345–51.

DeSalvo, L. 1999. *Writing as a Way of Healing: How Telling Our Stories Transforms Our Lives*. Boston: Beacon Press.

Domitrovich, C. E., R. C. Cortes, and M. T. Greenberg. 2007. "Improving Young Children's Social and Emotional Competence: A Randomized Trial of the Preschool 'PATHS' Curriculum." *The Journal of Primary Prevention* 28 (2): 67–91.

Dorado, J. S., M. Martinez, L. E. McArthur, and T. Leibovitz. 2016. "Healthy Environments and Response to Trauma in Schools (HEARTS): A Whole-School, Multi-Level, Prevention and Intervention Program for Creating Trauma-Informed, Safe and Supportive Schools." *School Mental Health* 8: 163–76. http://dx.doi.org/10.1007/s12310-016-9177-0.

Duane, A. 2022. "School-Based Trauma: A Scoping Review." *Journal of Trauma Studies in Education*.

Duane, A., A. E. Casimir, L. C. Mims, C. Kaler-Jones, and D. Simmons.

2021. "Beyond Deep Breathing: A New Vision for equitable, Culturally Responsive, and Trauma-Informed Mindfulness Practice." *Middle School Journal* 52 (3): 4–14.

Duane, A. and A. S. Venet 2022. "Thirteen Ways of Looking at Trauma: Problems and Possibilities in Trauma Theory for ELA Teachers." Champaign, IL: *National Council of Teachers of English.*

Durlak, J. A., A. B. Dymnicki, R. D. Taylor, R. P. Weissberg, K. B. Schellinger, D. Dubois, M. U. O'Brien, M. Lipsey, and M. Greenberg. 2007. Collaborative for Academic, Social, and Emotional Learning (CASEL).

Durlak, J. A., R. P. Weissberg, A. B. Dymnicki, R. D. Taylor, and K. B. Schellinger. 2011. "The Impact of Enhancing Students' Social and Emotional Learning: A Meta-Analysis of School-Based Universal Interventions." *Child Development* 82 (1): 405–32.

Dutro, E. 2011. "Writing Wounded: Trauma, Testimony, and Critical Witness in Literacy Classrooms." *English Education* 43 (2): 193–211.

———. 2019. *The Vulnerable Heart of Literacy: Centering Trauma as Powerful Pedagogy.* New York: Teachers College Press.

Felitti, V. J., R. F. Anda, D. Nordenberg, D. F. Williamson, A. M. Spitz, V. Edwards, M. P. Koss, and J. S. Marks. 1998. "Relationship of Childhood Abuse and Household Dysfunction to Many of the Leading Causes of Death in Adults: The Adverse Childhood Experiences (ACE) Study." *American Journal of Preventive Medicine* 14 (4): 245–58.

Ferlazzo, L. 2020. "Ways to Implement Restorative Practices in the Classroom." Education Week. https://www.edweek.org/teaching-learning/opinion-ways-to-implement-restorative-practices-in-the-classroom/2020/01.

Freire, P. 1964. *Pedagogy of the Oppressed.* New York: Bloomsbury.

Gaffney, C. 2019. "When Schools Cause Trauma." Learning for Justice. https://www.learningforjustice.org/magazine/summer-2019/when-schools-cause-trauma.

Garcia, A. R., M. Gupta, J. K. Greeson, A. Thompson, and C. DeNard. 2017. "Adverse Childhood Experiences Among Youth Reported to Child Welfare: Results from the National Survey of Child & Adolescent Well-Being." *Child Abuse & Neglect* 70: 292–302.

Gay, G., and K. Kirkland. 2003. "Developing Cultural Critical Consciousness and Self-Reflection in Preservice Teacher Education." *Theory into Practice* 42 (3): 181–87.

Gilliam, W. S. 2016. *Early Childhood Expulsions and Suspensions Undermine Our Nation's Most Promising Agent of Opportunity and Social Justice.* Moriah Group. www.the moriahgroup.com

Ginwright, S. 2018. "The Future of Healing: Shifting From Trauma Informed Care to Healing Centered Engagement." Medium. https://ginwright.medium.com/the-future-of-healing-shifting -from-trauma-informed-care-to-healing-centered-engagement -634f557ce69c.

Giordano, K., V. L. Interra, G. C. Stillo, A. T. Mims, and J. Block-Lerner. 2020. "Associations Between Child and Administrator Race and Suspension and Expulsion Rates in Community Childcare Programs." *Early Childhood Education Journal* 1–9.

Golberstein, E., H. Wen, and B. F. Miller. 2020. "Coronavirus Disease 2019 (COVID-19) and Mental Health for Children and Adolescents." *JAMA Pediatrics.*

Greene R. and J. S. Ablon. 2006. *Treating Explosive Kids: The Collaborative Problem-Solving Approach.* New York: Guilford Press.

Gregory, A., K. Clawson, A. Davis, and J. Gerewitz. 2016a. "The Promise of Restorative Practices to Transform Teacher-Student Relationships and Achieve Equity in School Discipline." *Journal of Educational and Psychological Consultation* 26 (4): 325–353.

Gregory, A., C. A. Hafen, E. Ruzek, A. Y. Mikami, J. P. Allen, and R. C. Pianta. 2016. "Closing the Racial Discipline Gap in Classrooms by Changing Teacher Practice." *School Psychology Review* 45(2): 171–91.

Haga, K. 2020. *Healing Resistance: A Radically Different Response to Harm.* Berkeley, CA: Parallax.

Halfon, N., K. Larson, M. Lu, E. Tullis, and S. Russ. 2014. "Life Course Health Development: Past, Present and Future." *Maternal and Child Health Journal* 18 (2): 344–65.

Hamre, B. K., and R. C. Pianta. 2005. "Can Instructional and Emotional Support in the First-Grade Classroom Make a Difference for Children at Risk of School Failure?" *Child Development* 76 (5): 949–67.

Harris, M., and R. D. Fallot. 2001. *Using Trauma Theory to Design Service Systems*. San Francisco: Jossey-Bass.

Harris, N. B. 2018. *The Deepest Well: Healing the Long-Term Effects of Childhood Adversity*. Boston: Houghton Mifflin Harcourt.

Harvard. n.d. "Project Implicit." www.implicit.harvard.edu.

Herman, J. 1992. *Trauma and Recovery: The Aftermath of Violence – from Domestic Abuse to Political Terror*. New York: Basic Books.

Herman, K. C., J. E. Hickmon-Rosa, and W. M. Reinke. 2018. "Empirically Derived Profiles of Teacher Stress, Burnout, Self-Efficacy, and Coping and Associated Student Outcomes." *Journal of Positive Behavior Interventions* 20 (2): 90–100.

Herman, K. C., and W. M. Reinke. 2014. *Stress Management for Teachers: A Proactive Guide*. New York: Guilford Publications.

Hirschberger, G. 2018. "Collective Trauma and the Social Construction of Meaning." *Front. Psychol.* 9:1441. doi: 10.3389/fpsyg.2018.01441

Hoglund, W. L., K. E. Klingle, and N. E. Hosan. 2015. "Classroom Risks and Resources: Teacher Burnout, Classroom Quality and Children's Adjustment in High Needs Elementary Schools." *Journal of School Psychology* 53 (5): 337–357.

Holliday, M. R., A. Cimetta, C. A. Cutshaw, D. Yaden, and R. W. Marx. 2014. "Protective Factors for School Readiness Among Children in Poverty." *Journal of Education for Students Placed at Risk (JESPAR)* 19 (3–4): 125–47.

Holmes, S. C., V. C. Facemire, and A. M. DaFonseca. 2016. "Expanding a Criterion for Posttraumatic Stress Disorder: Considering the Deleterious Impact of Oppression." *Traumatology* 22 (4): 314.

hooks, b. 2001. *All About Love: New Visions*. New York: William Morrow Paperbacks.

———. 2002. *Homemade Love*. Jump at the Sun.

———. 2003. *Teaching Community: A Pedagogy of Hope*, 1st ed. New York: Routledge.

————. 2009. *Teaching Critical Thinking: Practical Wisdom*. Routledge.

Howard, J. R., T. Milner-McCall, and T. C. Howard. 2020. *No More Teaching Without Positive Relationships*. Portsmouth, NH: Heinemann.

Isobel, S., M. Goodyear, and K. Foster. 2019. "Psychological Trauma in the Context of Familial Relationships: A Concept Analysis." *Trauma, Violence, & Abuse* 20 (4): 549–59.

Jones, D. E., M. Greenberg, and M. Crowley. 2015. "Early Social-Emotional Functioning and Public Health: The Relationship Between Kindergarten Social Competence and Future Wellness." *American Journal of Public Health* 105 (11): 2283–2290.

Joseph, G. E., and P. S. Strain. 2003. "Comprehensive Evidence-Based Social—Emotional Curricula for Young Children: An Analysis of Efficacious Adoption Potential." *Topics in Early Childhood Special Education* 23 (2): 62–73.

Kincade, L., C. Cook, and A. Goerdt. 2020. "Meta-Analysis and Common Practice Elements of Universal Approaches to Improving Student-Teacher Relationships." *Review of Educational Research* 90 (5): 710–48.

Ladson-Billings, G. 1995. "Toward a Theory of Culturally Relevant Pedagogy." *American Educational Research Journal* 32 (3): 465–491.

————. 2009. *The Dreamkeepers: Successful Teachers of African American Children*. Hoboken, NJ: John Wiley & Sons.

Lantieri, L. 2001. *Schools with Spirit: Nurturing the Inner Lives of Students and Teachers*. Boston: Beacon.

Lawson, G. M., M. E. McKenzie, K. D. Becker, L. Selby, and S. A. Hoover. 2019. "The Core Components of Evidence-Based Social Emotional Learning Programs." *Prevention Science* 20 (4): 457–467.

Le Guin, U. K. 2015. "106. A Child Who Survived." December 28. https://www.ursulakleguin.com/blog/106-a-child-who-survived.

Love, B. L. 2019. *We Want to Do More Than Survive: Abolitionist Teaching and the Pursuit of Educational Freedom*. Boston Beacon.

Magee, R.V. 2019. *The Inner Work of Racial Justice. Healing Ourselves and Transforming Our Communities Through Mindfulness*. London, UK: Penguin.

Maslach, C., W. B. Schaufeli, and M. P. Leiter. 2001. "Job Burnout." *Annual Review of Psychology* 52: 397–422.

McClelland, M. M., S. L. Tominey, S. A. Schmitt, and R. Duncan. 2017. "SEL Interventions in Early Childhood." *The Future of Children* 33–47.

McEwen, B. S. 2007. "Physiology and Neurobiology of Stress and Adaptation: Central Role of the Brain." *Physiological Reviews* 87 (3): 873–904.

McIntyre, E. M., C. N. Baker, S. Overstreet, and The New Orleans Trauma-Informed Schools Learning Collaborative. 2019. "Evaluating Foundational Professional Development Training for Trauma-Informed Approaches in Schools." *Psychological Services* 16 (1): 95–102. doi: 10.1037/ser0000312.

Menschner, C., and A. Maul. 2016. *Key Ingredients for Successful Trauma-Informed Care Implementation.* Trenton, NJ: Center for Health Care Strategies, Incorporated.

Merrick, M. T., D. C. Ford, K. A. Ports, and A. S. Guinn. 2018. "Prevalence of Adverse Childhood Experiences from the 2011–2014 Behavioral Risk Factor Surveillance System in 23 States." *JAMA Pediatrics* 172 (11): 1038–1044.

Milner H. R. IV. 2012. "Beyond a Test Score: Explaining Opportunity Gaps in Educational Practice." *Journal of Black Studies* 43 (6): 693–718.

Minor, C. 2019. *We Got This: Equity, Access and the Quest to be Who Our Students Need Us to Be.* Portsmouth, NH: Heinemann.

Montgomery, C., and A. Rupp. 2005. "A Meta-Analysis for Exploring the Diverse Causes and Effects of Stress in Teachers." *Canadian Journal of Education* 28: 458–86.

Morgenstern, J. 2018. "Getting Your Mojo Back." https://www.juliemorgenstern.com/tips-tools-blog/2022/11/1/getting -your-mojo-back?utm_source=Weekly+Video+Audience&utm _campaign=ec02acbc6b-EMAIL_CAMPAIGN_2018_05_22 _COPY_01&utm_medium=email&utm_term=0_e5777f2dbd -ec02acbc6b-310007141.

Morris, M. 2016. *Pushout: The Criminalization of Black Girls in Schools.* New York: The New Press.

National Association of School Psychologists. 2019. *Prejudice, Discrimination, and Racism (Position Statement).* Bethesda, MD: Author.

Oberle, E., and K. A. Schonert-Reichl. 2016. "Stress Contagion in the Classroom? The Link Between Classroom Teacher Burnout and Morning Cortisol in Elementary School Students." *Social Science & Medicine* 159: 30–37.

Okun, T. 2021. "White Supremacy Culture Characteristics." White Supremacy Culture. https://www.whitesupremacyculture.info /characteristics.html.

Overstreet, S., and S. M. Chafouleas. 2016. "Trauma-Informed Schools: Introduction to the Special Issue." *School Mental Health* 8 (1): 1–6.

Overstreet, S., and T. Mathews. 2011. "Challenges Associated with Exposure to Chronic Trauma: Using a Public Health Framework to Foster Resilient Outcomes Among Youth." *Psychology in the Schools* 48 (7): 738–754.

Palmer, P. J. 1998. *The Courage to Teach: Exploring the Inner Landscape of a Teacher's Life*. Hoboken, NJ: John Wiley & Sons.

Pat-Horenczyk, R., and D. Brom. 2007. "The Multiple Faces of Post-Traumatic Growth." *Applied Psychology* 56 (3): 379–85.

Perfect, M. M., M. R. Turley, J. S. Carlson, J. Yohanna, and M. P. Saint Gilles. 2016. "School-Related Outcomes of Traumatic Event Exposure and Traumatic Stress Symptoms in Students: A Systematic Review of Research from 1990 to 2015." *School Mental Health* 8 (1): 7–43.

Pickford, D. Y., T. L. Hill, P. G. Arora, and C. N. Baker. 2021. "Prevention of Conduct Problems in Integrated Pediatric Primary Care." In *Handbook of Evidence-Based Prevention of Behavioral Disorders in Integrated Care*, 193–220. Cham, Switzerland: Springer.

Porche, M. V., D. M. Costello, and M. Rosen-Reynoso. 2016. "Adverse Family Experiences, Child Mental Health, and Educational Outcomes for a National Sample of Students." *School Mental Health* 8 (1): 44–60.

Porche, M. V., L. R. Fortuna, J. Lin, and M. Alegria. 2011. "Childhood Trauma and Psychiatric Disorders as Correlates of School Dropout in a National Sample of Young Adults." *Child Development* 82 (3): 982–98.

Richards, A. S. 2020. *Raising Free People: Unschooling as Liberation and Healing Work*. Binghampton, NY: PM Press.

Roorda, D. L., H. M. Koomen, J. L. Spilt, and F. J. Oort. 2011. "The Influence of Affective Teacher–Student Relationships on Students' School Engagement and Achievement: A Meta-Analytic Approach." *Review of Educational Research* 81 (4): 493–529.

Rossen, E., ed. 2020. *Supporting and Educating Traumatized Students: A Guide for School-Based Professionals*. New York: Oxford University Press.

Rossen, E., and K. C. Cowan. 2012. *A Framework for School-Wide Bullying Prevention and Safety* [Brief]. Bethesda, MD: National Association of School Psychologists.

Ruiz, D. M. Jr. 2017. *The Mastery of Self: A Toltec Guide to Personal Freedom*. San Antonio, TX: Hierophant Publishing.

Rumi, M. J. 2011. "The Guest House." Poetry.Com. https://www. poetry.com/poem/28064/the-guest-house.

Safe Schools NOLA. 2019. *Strengthening Relationships*. Unpublished curriculum.

Saleem, F. T., R. E. Anderson, and M. Williams. 2020. "Addressing the 'Myth' of Racial Trauma: Developmental and Ecological Considerations for Youth of Color." *Clinical Child and Family Psychology Review* 23 (1): 1–14.

Sandilos, L. E., S. E. Rimm-Kaufman, and J. J. Cohen. 2017. "Warmth and Demand: The Relation Between Students' Perceptions of the Classroom Environment and Achievement Growth." *Child Development* 88 (4): 1321–37.

Seng, J., and Group, Ca. 2019. "From Fight or Flight, Freeze or Faint, to 'Flow': Identifying a Concept to Express a Positive Embodied Outcome of Trauma Recovery." *Journal of the American Psychiatric Nurses Association* 25 (3): 200–207.

Shalaby, C. 2017. *Trouble Makers: Lessons in Freedom from Young Children at School*. New York: The New Press.

Sharif, M. A., C. Mogilner, and H.E. Hershfield. 2021. "Having too little or too much time is linked to lower subjective well-being." *Journal of Personality and Social Psychology*, 121(4), 933-947. https://doi.org/10.1037/pspp0000391.

Shonkoff, J. P. 2016. "Capitalizing on Advances in Science to Reduce the Health Consequences of Early Childhood Adversity." *JAMA Pediatrics* 170 (10): 1003–1007.

Silva, K. M., T. L. Spinrad, N. Eisenberg, M. J. Sulik, C. Valiente, S. Huerta, … and School Readiness Consortium. 2011. "Relations of Children's Effortful Control and Teacher–Child Relationship Quality to School Attitudes in a Low-Income Sample." *Early Education & Development* 22 (3): 434–60.

Simmons, D. 2021. "Why SEL Alone Isn't Enough". ASCD. October 7. https://www.ascd.org/el/articles/why-sel-alone-isnt-enough.

Simonsen, B., S. Fairbanks, A. Briesch, D. Myers, and G. Sugai. 2008. "Evidence-Based Practices in Classroom Management: Considerations for Research to Practice." *Education and Treatment of Children* 351–80.

Skinner, B. F. 1965. *Science and Human Behavior.* New York: Simon and Schuster.

Spencer, M. B., D. Dupree, and T. Hartmann. 1997. "A Phenomenological Variant of Ecological Systems Theory (PVEST): A Self-Organization Perspective in Context." *Development and Psychopathology* 9 (4): 817–833.

Stamm, B. H. 2009–2012. "Professional Quality of Life Scale (PROQOL): Compassion Satisfaction and Fatigue. Version 5." https://img1.wsimg.com/blobby/go/dfc1e1a0-a1db-4456-9391-18746725179b/downloads/ProQOL_5_English_Self-Score.pdf?ver=1657301051771.

Stamm, B. H., H. E. Stamm, A. C. Hudnall, and C. Higson-Smith. 2004. "Considering a Theory of Cultural Trauma and Loss." *Journal of Loss and Trauma* 9 (1): 89–111.

Starecheski, L. 2015. "Take the ACE Quiz—and Learn What It Means and Doesn't Mean." NPR. https://www.npr.org/sections/health-shots/2015/03/02/387007941/take-the-ace-quiz-and-learn-what-it-does-and-doesnt-mean.

Substance Abuse and Mental Health Services Administration. 2014. *SAMHSA's Concept of Trauma and Guidance for a Trauma-Informed Approach.* www.samhsa.gov.

Sue, D. W. 2001. "Multidimensional Facets of Cultural Competence." *The Counseling Psychologist* 29 (6): 790–821.

Sue, D. W., S. Alsaidi, M. N. Awad, E. Glaeser, C. Z. Calle, and N. Mendez. 2019. "Disarming Racial Microaggressions: Microintervention Strategies for Targets, White Allies, and Bystanders." *American Psychologist* 74 (1): 128.

Taylor, S. R. (@sonyareneetaylor). 2020. "We Will Not Go Back to Normal. Normal Never Was." [Photograph]. Instagram, April 2. Instagram. https://www.instagram.com/p/B-fc3ejAlvd/?hl=en.

Tenenbaum, H. R., and M. D. Ruck. 2007. "Are Teachers' Expectations Different for Racial Minority Than for European American Students? A Meta-Analysis." *Journal of Educational Psychology* 99 (2): 253.

Thomas, M. S., S. Crosby, and J. Vanderhaar. 2019. "Trauma-Informed Practices in Schools Across Two Decades: An Interdisciplinary Review of Research." *Review of Research in Education* 43 (1): 422–452.

Upshur, C. C., M. Wenz-Gross, C. Rhoads, M. Heyman, Y. Yoo, and G. Sawosik. 2019. "A Randomized Efficacy Trial of the Second Step Early Learning (SSEL) Curriculum." *Journal of Applied Developmental Psychology* 62: 145–59.

Vandenbroucke, L., J. Spilt, K. Verschueren, C. Piccinin, and D. Baeyens. 2018. "The Classroom as a Developmental Context for Cognitive Development: A Meta-Analysis on the Importance of Teacher–Student Interactions for Children's Executive Functions." *Review of Educational Research* 88 (1): 125–64.

Venet, A. S. 2021. *Equity-Centered Trauma-Informed Education.* New York: W. W. Norton.

von der Embse, N., L. Rutherford, A. Mankin, and A. Jenkins. 2018. "Demonstration of a Trauma-Informed Assessment to Intervention Model in a Large Urban School District." *School Mental Health.* https://doi.org/10.1007/s12310-018-9294-z.

von der Embse, N., S. V. Ryan, T. Gibbs, and A. Mankin. 2019. "Teacher Stress Interventions: A Systematic Review." *Psychology in the Schools* 56 (8): 1328–1343.

Vygotsky, L. S., R. E. van der Veer, J. E. Valsiner, and T. T. Prout. 1994. *The Vygotsky Reader.* Oxford, UK and Cambridge, USA: Blackwell Publishers.

Webster-Stratton, C., M. J. Reid, and M. Hammond. 2004. "Treating Children with Early-Onset Conduct Problems: Intervention Outcomes for Parent, Child, and Teacher Training." *Journal of Clinical Child and Adolescent Psychology* 33 (1): 105–24.

Webster-Stratton, C., M. J. Reid, and M. Stoolmiller. 2008. "Preventing Conduct Problems and Improving School Readiness: Evaluation of the Incredible Years Teacher and Child Training Programs in High-Risk Schools." *Journal of Child Psychology and Psychiatry* 49 (5): 471–88.

Wittich, C., C. Rupp, S. Overstreet, C. N. Baker, and the New Orleans Trauma-Informed Schools Learning Collaborative. 2020. "Barriers and Facilitators of the Implementation of Trauma-Informed Schools." *Research and Practice in the Schools* 7: 33–48.

Winfrey, O., and B. D. Perry. 2021. *What Happened to You? Conversations on Trauma, Resilience, and Healing.* New York: Flatiron Books.

Winn, M. T. 2020. *Justice on Both Sides: Transforming Education Through Restorative Justice.* Cambridge, MA: Harvard Education Press.

Wolpow, R., M. M. Johnson, R. Hertel, and S. O. Kincaid. 2009. *The Heart of Learning and Teaching: Compassion, Resiliency, and Academic Success.* Office of Superintendent of Public Instruction (OSPI) Compassionate Schools.

Wolynn, M. 2016. *It Didn't Start with You: How Inherited Family Trauma Shapes Who We are and How to End the Cycle.* London, UK: Penguin Books.